AMERICA'S GREAT RIVER JOURNEYS

TERRAIN ELEVATION

- 8,000 feet
- 6,000 feet
- 4,000 feet
- 2,000 feet
- 1,000 feet
- 500 feet

RIVERS

- River Journeys
- Other Major Rivers

0   200 Miles

AMERICA'S GREAT
RIVER JOURNEYS

AMERICA'S GREAT

RIVER JOURNEYS

50 CANOE, KAYAK, AND RAFT ADVENTURES

Text and Photographs by

TIM PALMER

Foreword by **RICHARD BANGS**

RIZZOLI
NEW YORK

New York · Paris · London · Milan

American Rivers
Rivers Connect Us

CONTENTS

FOREWORD   by Richard Bangs

We shall not cease from exploration, and the end
of all our exploring will be to arrive where we started
and know the place for the first time.   T. S. ELIOT

A river is a poem that pours a dream, conveying us into realms magical and phantasmagoric. Every environment is touched, from desert to montane to forest, field, and fantasy; to the grand, the perilous, the irregular, and the breathtaking. Angels meet devils on rivers. Wildlife is drawn to its fundamentals. People as well, but also for what rivers do to those who let go of the shore and surrender to the flow and flurry of feral water. A wild river is about transformation, not transportation. We are all different for a river trip, more connected, more aware, more appreciative. And, not to be discounted or eddied out, there is the personal reason why a river makes sense: the vitalizing gift of crisp, clear water; the splendid frisson that comes with gliding by the edge; and the moments we feel most alive when we can imagine our own demise.

I began my career as a guide on the Colorado River in the Grand Canyon when but nineteen years of age, a summer thing while in college. It was such a powerful experience, though, the axis of my identity spun to a new meridian, pointing away from law school and toward Africa and its spate of unrun wild rivers. I started a company, Sobek Expeditions, dedicated to riding the dragon waters all over the world. But, years later, when I came home to nest in California, I once again began to run some in the galaxies of rivers of America. My travels had given me a new appreciation for the variety and quality of the flows and fluxes, a new awe for the star power of nearby currents whose essence and magnetism Tim Palmer has expertly captured in this book.

Once home, I could not resist the flame of the Chattooga, a legendary river that divides South Carolina and Georgia with renowned whitewater and beauty. As we approached the tongue of the first major rapid, I pointed the raft like an arrow downstream and hung on. But a mad side wave pushed me off my path. I felt my body tense like a drawn bow. I watched in horror as the water broke around my paddle like glass as I tried to straighten the boat. I couldn't correct it, and we washed into the hole at an angle. The raft buckled and kicked and rose to ride the hydraulic, and then it stalled. I felt the torque and rattle in my bones, my heart feathering through my breast. I slammed my blade like a beaver tail into the curl. If the raft slipped back, we would be caught in the death trap. We hung at the rounded crest of the hydraulic for an eternity—the raft and the wave like two wrestlers locked in a trembling stalemate, waiting for one to give. The fabric beneath us seemed to shudder as though about to explode, and then suddenly we shot to the other side, safe and sound.

We purled into the temple of the sublime, which can be reached, in one way or another, on every wild river that remains, whether its thrill be highly pitched or quietly comforting.

I was challenged, on that trip, to follow what Tim, in his epilogue here, says is the first rule when going on a river trip: to keep people safe from the river. And then he adds that the first rule *after* the trip is to keep the river safe from people. Every river in this good book is threatened, by dams, diversion schemes, development, the unwinding of protection, even global warming. Only people can destroy these arteries of life and joy; only people can save them. And the first step in securing the future for a river is to experience it, as then it becomes personal, like a family member, and its worth inherent. Then, a river is like a relative, and when threatened or imperiled, voices are raised, wallets opened, actions taken, and, if lucky, the stream is saved to run another day.

May every river in this book be so fortunate. Tim has assembled a testament to the finest of America and a wish list of the fifty best river journeys one might imagine. Each current dreams the one to follow. Everything that is romantic, gentle, terrifying, tranquil, turbulent,

refreshing, and idyllic in the whole wide world of nature is united here for our reward and satisfaction, all with the fever and the dizziness and the uproar and the tohubohu of happiness.

A guide to be trusted, Tim has captured all of this—and more—in his vivid prose and breathlessly beautiful photos. I urge you to read, to look, to dream, and to follow Tim's advice to enrich your life by experiencing these rivers and thereby reunite yourself with the real and natural world.

As Tim shows, the rivers of America provide vital perspective and bearings, feed the springs of reverence and affection, quicken our sense of wonder, provoke the imaginings of eternity and infinity, and inspire us to great deeds of preservation.

A life pursuing these fifty journeys would be a life well worth living. Tim has shown the way. I, for one, am eager to follow, and will begin by turning this page.

Whisking travelers downstream, the Delaware River of Pennsylvania, New York, and New Jersey introduces many people to the joys of river travel with journeys as short as a few hours and as long as two weeks. FOLLOWING SPREAD: The Green River winds through Desolation Canyon in Utah.

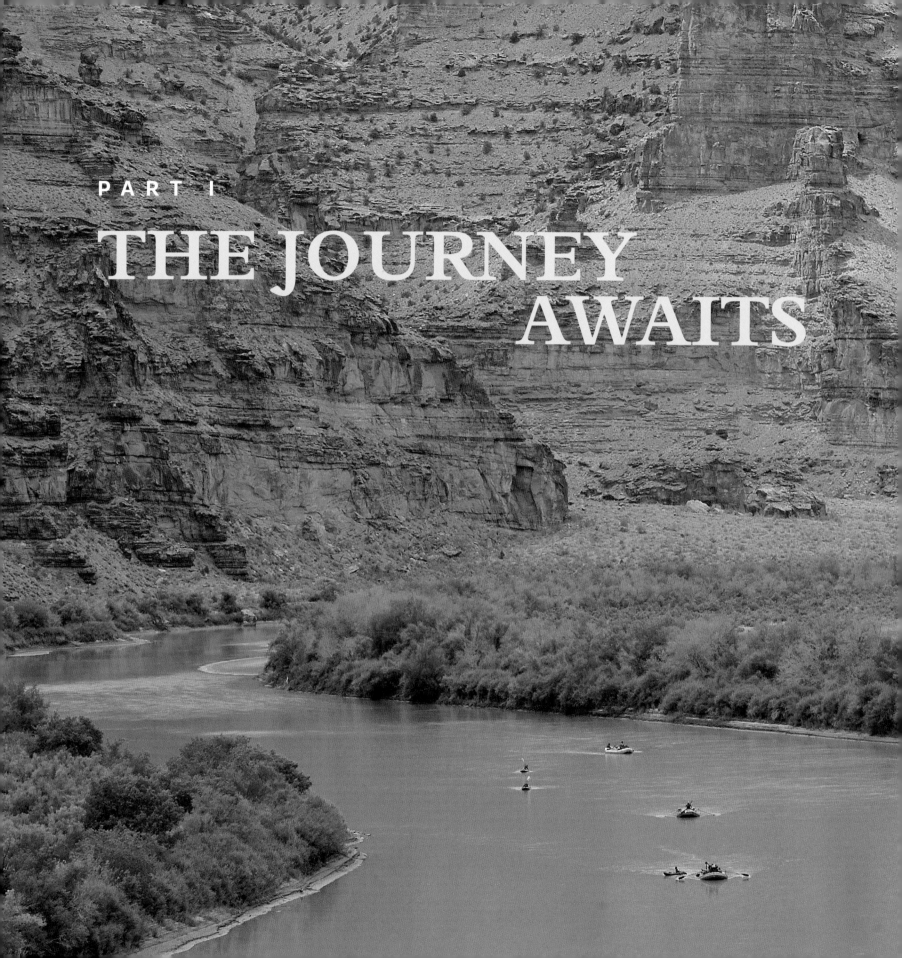

PART I

THE JOURNEY AWAITS

FOLLOW THE RIVER

Rivers wind and plunge as pathways of adventure, of exploration, and of nature, and river journeys offer a view not seen through a windshield.

Traveling on rivers in a canoe, raft, or kayak is a pastime and passion of many Americans and also of visitors from around the world. Drifting with the current draws us into the unknown—an incredibly beautiful unknown. Both the serenity of mirroring pools and the rush of explosive rapids stir the body, the psyche, and the spirit.

Part of the fascination with river trips comes simply from the joy that they offer to all. And it's not just about us. Rivers are home to fish and wildlife, and in traveling on these waterways we can see how important and fruitful they are. Rivers are animated blue-green ribbons of life that intertwine whole landscapes, regions, and states. Rivers cool us on hot days, take us to enchanting places, and in quiet moments instill or stir thoughts that probe to the core of vital experiences, meanings, and mysteries.

Another part of rivers' appeal may owe to deep evolutionary linkages. Our bodies are sixty-seven percent water, and every drop of it comes from a river or from groundwater that's intimately tied to the surface flow. The connection that many of us feel to the flow of rivers is no mystery; they literally run in our arteries and veins.

The inexpressible, unexplainable satisfaction, pleasure, and thrill that many people feel simply by standing alongside a beautiful river goes deep into our history and our consciousness. Rivers contain life, they support it, and they symbolize it in metaphors and associations that poets, songwriters, and novelists have drawn upon for the ages. At the turn of the twentieth century, America's first great nature guardian, John Muir, aptly wrote, "The rivers flow not past, but through us." With similar thoughts, author Florence Williams, in 2017, wrote about sojourns through the natural world in her pathbreaking book, *The Nature Fix*, reflecting that "these trips can rearrange our very core, cata-lyzing our hopes and dreams, filling us with awe and human connection and offering a reassurance of our place in the universe."

Let gravity do the work on the river of our choice! Easily taken for granted, floating on the current is a pleasure unlike any other. We drift without effort, as if airborne in slow-motion flight above the rocks and terrain beneath us. This can be done in utter silence and relaxation as we watch the river bottom and shorelines go by, and there's something special and serene about doing that for not just a moment or an hour, but for days.

At other times, river running requires a burst of energy to paddle or row away from danger or to follow the liquid path through a maze of hazards. It must be done right! This requires maximum use of both mind and body in a way that activates every nerve and muscle, and that fills the moment to the brim. Sensing unknown threats ahead, boaters might stop to scout. Walking down the shore, we see and appraise the difficulties, consider the risks and consequences, and devise a plan for overcoming them all. Then we launch, knowing what we must do. There's no room for the thoughts, worries, or commitments that we otherwise shoulder. We face nonnegotiable demands to paddle forward, to angle left or right, and to pull on the oars at precisely the required instant.

A remarkable rush of satisfaction comes from this total engagement. The rest of the world disappears. And so when it later reappears, it somehow seems fresher and new. We're ready to confront the next challenge—in the river or in our lives.

River travelers encounter numberless pleasures, but also headwinds, foul weather, rocky campsites, and tiring days to reach our destinations. The efforts and discomforts might be great, but the rewards are far greater.

Rivers deliver us to both rugged canyons and lyrical valleys, to wilderness that's untouched, and also to the nation's esteemed heritage of

The Green River in Lodore Canyon of Colorado entices boaters onward while the blue tint of twilight reflects on the river.

historic landmarks. In their timelessness, the currents of today can take us back in time. On the water and away from the road, we can imagine the past few centuries by following the paths of Native Americans and the explorations of Lewis and Clark. For that matter, we can sense a flashback to the ice ages, to the dawn of humankind, and to the primeval emergence of mountains whose profiles have been shaped by the water's timeless flow with its power to move sand, stones, and boulders, gradually but inevitably recontouring the earth to the features we see today.

River trips offer visions not just of the past and present, but also of the future. A fate without strong connections and visceral attachments to the natural world would be doomed. By joining the flow and appreciating its beauty, we make those connections. We embrace those attachments.

On rivers, we can experience the allure of Edenic nature, available to all who seek an antidote to the cluttered artifacts of civilization, the din of traffic, and the stress of a world that seems, at times, to have gone mad.

River travel offers real, authentic experience. It's not about vicarious escapes, contrived appearances, or consumerism. Paddling or rowing, we guide our own boat, with our own muscles, wits, and judgments. We choose where we're going to live each night by selecting our own campsite, much like our nomadic ancestors did for millennia. Then we unload our gear, pitch our tent, cook dinner, lean back, and watch the stars fall into the sky. Finally we lie under a dome of sycamore or cottonwood limbs, suspended at our precious home along the edge of the river as though floating on the waters of the universe all through the night.

River trips are microcosms of life itself with its mix of security and risks, comforts and hardships, escapes and returns.

These journeys can be done with family, friends, like-minded people, total strangers, and all of the above. Being out there, and connected in a common endeavor, we work together, share the duties and rewards, and get to know each other under conditions that not only allow, but also require it.

Rivers come from mountain or upland sources and they swell to grand finales at the edge of the sea. In between—if we're willing to go—they sweep us up in journeys to the heart of America.

Short outings of a day or two can open our eyes to something new and revealing. And that might be enough. But even better, we can pack our canoes or rafts for days, weeks, or a month if we have the time and

Autumn's colors brighten the White Mountains above the Saco River in New Hampshire.

inclination. These longer trips invite our own Huckleberry Finn odyssey and our own extended escape from the world we know.

While any day on a river can be exquisite, staying out for the long haul transcends normal notions of recreation and takes on the quality of *living* there. We might even call it *re-creation*. Immersed in different measures of time, we enter the river's ancient rhythms, its ebb and flow, its morning calm followed by afternoon wind, its pool and riffle sequence, over and over. There's simply nothing else like it.

Some rivers demand expert skills, and some can be run by beginners or parents with small children. Short outings are simpler to arrange than long ones, yet long ones offer rewards like nothing else in life, and so in this book I cover the possibilities for many types of trips.

For rivers with threatening rapids or logistical complications, some people will prefer to go with a professional guide, leaving formidable issues of safety, skill, permits, shuttles, and food to them. An outfitted trip might be a perfect introduction to the joys of river running, or it might serve as a springboard for a traveler to go out on their own once they get the drift, so to speak.

One thing I don't want to do in this book is spoil the adventure by revealing too much. Facing the unknown is half the fun! My goal is simply to point where you might want to go—to identify outstanding rivers and describe the big draw, whether it's whitewater and wilderness or perhaps security and comforts while still getting the river fix. I'll reveal the lengths of trips possible, flag some of the risks that might arise, and lightly blaze a path to splendid new worlds apart from those we normally inhabit. The choices will be up to you in deciding whether to explore on your own or go with a guide, to launch for a day or a week, to stay near home or head for distant horizons. Part of the adventure is in finding your own route through the rapids and in meeting each challenge as it arises—all in the spirit of adventure—mild, moderate, or extreme.

One of the most satisfying aspects of river trips is that we don't have to travel the globe to find what we seek. For many people, fabulous journeys lie close to home, where we can embark without driving for days or flying far. In the age of the climate crisis, here's a mode of travel and a path to adventure that doesn't have to burn a lot of gas or jet fuel. Of course, we first have to get to the river. But then, once we've launched, the energy source for all we see and do is the flow of water powered by the simple pull of gravity, day after day.

Some of the trips described here transect entire mountain ranges. Others run the length of spacious valleys, through swamps, or across prairies. A few go the whole way to the ocean. All take us to places that seduce in their beauty, that beg to be admired, that deserve to be protected. Once we go, these rivers become places we can call our own, even though they might seem like the most exotic outposts on earth.

Whatever your experience, skills, and getaway options happen to be, come along, right now. Join this tour of fifty great rivers that await all who are curious and all who are eager to see our earth as never before.

OPPOSITE: White-tailed deer browse the shoreline of the Delaware River in northeastern Pennsylvania. Up to seventy-five percent of wildlife depend on riverfronts at one time or another for habitat.

River trips offer not only excitement and adventure, but also the chance to relax while surrounded by the beauty of flowing waters, such as the Grande Ronde in Oregon (top right). Independent paddlers stage expeditions on their own. Author Tim Palmer and his wife Ann Vileisis have rigged their canoe and raft for a week on the Grande Ronde in Oregon and Washington (bottom right).

CHOOSE YOUR RIVER

Perhaps you have a river or a vision of free-flowing travel in mind. Maybe it's the ultimate big-water journey down the Colorado River through the Grand Canyon. Or maybe it's the American River's burst of rapids not far from Sacramento, the serene Suwannee in the Deep South, the Missouri riffling across the Plains, the North Woods Allagash, the New River in the misty folds of the Appalachians, or the Potomac with national heritage written all over it. This book will go to each of those, and beyond.

From a remarkable nationwide estate of rivers, I've considered the most beautiful, the most enticing for camping, and the most natural. I eliminated reaches that have large dams and impassable rapids, and I favored those with easy access and shorelines in public ownership. I looked for trips in all regions of the country, and for excursions of varied lengths—a few hours to a month.

For some people, a single day on the water will be perfect. For others, a weekend will mean big adventure. Beyond that, a week or more can offer an eye-opening, mind-clearing, spirit-nourishing expedition to be remembered forever.

I must admit that, after fifty years of avid river travel, I'm hard pressed to identify only fifty outstanding American trips. There are more! It's tempting, for example, to highlight fifty rivers for their whitewater excitement alone.

Instead, and thinking of everyone, I sought rivers of varying types. Some people are drawn to the thrill of gradient or, then again, to the solace of a gentle flow. Maybe the green shores of the Appalachians or Pacific Northwest will resonate, or maybe it will be the golden glow of desert canyons in the Southwest. The varied intrinsic qualities of rivers overlap in many cases, but in this book I've organized the possibilities by region, and I've included river trips of four different types.

First, the American classics. These are destination journeys that draw people from all over the country and beyond, and they include some of the greatest adventures and scenic extravaganzas on earth. With overnight travel—up to a week or more—these rivers offer spectacular beauty and escape at a grand and orchestrated scale. Owing to the geography of wildness and to the patterns of land development in America, these rivers are found among public lands of the West. The Salmon in Idaho, Rogue in Oregon, Tuolumne in California, and Colorado through the Grand Canyon are among these magnificent escapes.

Second, we have exhilarating whitewater. The rush of a foaming rapid is a compelling lure to both seasoned and aspiring adventurers. The classic trips mentioned above offer some of America's criterion whitewater, but in this second category I include trips of one day. Big on thrills, they appeal to rafters and kayakers with advanced skills and perhaps to expert canoeists, but also to others electing to tap the expertise of a professional guide. Visit the incredible Chattooga of Georgia, Gauley of West Virginia, Youghiogheny of Pennsylvania, Hudson of New York, Arkansas of Colorado, White Salmon of Washington, and others.

Third, and my personal passion, are river trips of epic long length. Get on the water and go, go, go! The magic of river travel effervesces all the more when you stay out longer. Though some of the classic runs discussed above fall within this extended-trip category, many of the long outings featured in this book are easier, with only a few big rapids or, in some cases, none at all. They are dam-free for 100 miles or more. Even without going to Alaska, three trips of 400 miles are possible. These long outings to places we've never been can become great expeditions and expansive journeys of discovery.

Although some of these extended trips traverse civilized and cultured terrain, they offer an option for adventure that's subtly but importantly different from the most hyped whitewater or the most enticingly popular wilderness. On the famously classic trips, such as the Salmon or Rogue,

The Colorado River in Arizona's Grand Canyon is classic among American river trips. None compare to its combination of towering sandstone walls, big whitewater, and long wilderness mileage through the southwestern desert.

you'll likely see other people traveling just like yourself, and you'll camp at established sites occupied nearly every night in summer. But on many of the long-distance trips that I feature, such as Oregon's Umpqua, you'll encounter fewer boaters or maybe none. Even though more homes and roads are seen along the shores, the path downriver often feels more pioneering because so few people are boating there. Simply finding a place to sleep at night where there are no established campsites can become an adventure in its own right.

For the varied rewards of a long trip, try the Delaware for 200 miles, or the Willamette through the heartland of Oregon, or the Green through the red-rock canyons of Utah. Consider an incomparably wild multiweek expedition in Alaska with unmatched grandeur and the edginess of formidable weather, distance, bugs, and bears.

None of this is to say that every hour on the water will be spectacular. In fact, some of the appeal to the long trips is the satisfaction of paddling mile after mile through landscapes whose beauty is ordinary, to small towns with the chance to stop for lunch, and among pastoral hillsides or everyday woodlots with wildness at the microscale. Most of the long trips featured here can also be subdivided into shorter sojourns of a week, a weekend, or a day, and so they fit here not only as epic journeys, but also as our fourth type of river.

In this final group are sweet floats that are not so classic, not so adrenaline pumping, not so long. But they call with a special charm, and they appeal especially to boaters without expert skills, plus those wanting ready access for trips close to home. Consider the Saco in the White Mountains of New Hampshire, the Clarion through the wooded wilds of Pennsylvania, and the Yakima within the basalt canyons of Washington. Among the four types of rivers I've described here, this list is the most subjective because hundreds of streams could be recommended. I've selected outings that always leave me with fond memories and the urge to return.

In this book's fifty river journey narratives, I sometimes mention additional reaches nearby. More information about these, and others, is available in guidebooks cited in the back of this book.

Whatever your needs and desires, look at my map of our flowing waters, or just imagine all the blue lines curving across the landscape,

The Rogue River offers 157 miles of free-flowing travel from placid pools to white-knuckle rapids among the Cascade and Coast Mountains of Oregon. Driftboats here are favored by salmon anglers as the lower river slips through cool morning fog.

and allow yourself to dream. What would you see if you went there and followed the current wherever it flows? Where do those rivers come from? Where do they go? And to advance a step further, could your life change—with some welcome reorientation, whether subtle or profound—as a result of going out and joining the flow of a river? Time and again, people coming off a memorable outing comment heartfully and honestly, "That trip changed my life."

The adventure begins when you kick off from shore, dip a paddle or oar into the water, and eye the next bend downstream with a heightened sense of anticipation. All that and more await with any river you choose.

The Arkansas River of Colorado is the penultimate Rocky Mountain stream for running rapids. Four exhilarating sections spanning 100 miles thrill rafters and kayakers and receive more whitewater paddling use than any other river in the nation.

FOLLOWING SPREAD: The Klamath River rushes through rugged uplifts and deep forests of the Siskiyou and Coast Mountains in Northern California and offers the West Coast's longest dam-free river trip—nearly 200 miles through mostly undeveloped terrain.

ON THE WATER

Running rivers is fun, but just like crossing the street, whitewater and other aspects of outdoor trips can be hazardous to one degree or another. People traveling on a commercially outfitted trip will sensibly trust their guide regarding many matters of safety and judgment. Most guides are licensed, and most outfitters are diligent about safety and have excellent records of performance. Lists of responsible outfitters are available from the government agencies in charge of managing each river. These river stewards include the U.S. Forest Service, Bureau of Land Management (BLM), National Park Service, U.S. Fish and Wildlife Service, and a few state parks departments.

Boaters traveling on their own will, of course, assume all responsibility for their own safety. That's part of the fun and adventure! But for all, accurate assessment of potential hazards must be taken seriously.

Regardless of anything that any guidebook or advisor says, river runners need to know about their own limitations and about the conditions of water and weather at the time of their outing. Because readers here represent a wide and unknown range of abilities, information in this book should not be construed as a recommendation for any particular person to travel on the rivers described. In other words, information here is no substitute for common sense, prudence, experience, training, skill, adequate equipment, safe levels of flow, and competent personal assessment of dangers.

Judgments of hazards, even in the official international ratings of whitewater difficulty, vary with the individual. Fluctuations in water level and weather can alter risks greatly from assessments covered here or elsewhere, and hazards such as fallen logs or landslides can happen at any time and change conditions dramatically.

Being safe requires not only the ability to cope with dangers as they arise, but even more the ability to identify potential dangers before

Canoes are elegant craft for both gentle and swift currents. Here in a canoe designed for whitewater, author Tim Palmer navigates the Narrows of the Grande Ronde River in Washington.

they occur. Get the necessary instruction for your activity. Paddling clubs, kayak schools, the American Canoe Association, Outward Bound, the National Outdoor Leadership School, and independent professionals offer training courses, and much—or all—can be learned from competent friends and instruction books. All boaters should read the Safety Code of American Whitewater, available online, and follow it. All this information is important, but nothing takes the place of experience that builds incrementally to the challenges at hand.

A critical choice for any trip—and perhaps for an entire relationship with river running—is to choose your craft. Canoes, kayaks, inflatable kayaks (I-Ks), rafts, and dories are all capable boats.

Canoes are elegant in design, suited to many people for calm or riffling waters and also to the skilled paddler in models streamlined for running rapids. Full-sized canoes can carry substantial amounts of gear. Their grace and shape run deep in our heritage going back to birchbark vessels of the Iroquois and Chippewa.

For many people, kayaks are easier to paddle and, once the technique is mastered, they're ideal for heavier whitewater because breaking waves don't fill the boat with water the way they can do to an open canoe. But these smaller craft carry far less gear, you sit lower, and it's harder to get in and out of them.

Inflatable kayaks are more forgiving than hard-shell canoes or kayaks, with less consequence in glancing blows to rocks. They're more stable, less likely to tip over, and easier to master without a lot of practice. They're also much easier to store and transport, and lightweight models can be carried in a backpack to truly remote rivers. For fit people, an I-K is also easy to reboard if you flip over. But unlike a hard-shell kayak, inflatables cannot be turned upright with an "Eskimo" roll, and they're less maneuverable in the hands of a skilled paddler.

Rafts are more accommodating than canoes or kayaks with their ability to bounce or slide off rocks, their greater freeboard to plunge through larger rapids, their calming stability, and their capacity to carry lots of gear. Rafts are either rowed by one person sitting in the middle and facing downstream or by a crew of paddlers sitting on each side and taking orders from a guide in the back. Driftboats or dories can also carry gear through big-volume whitewater. They keep people drier than rafts do, and are favored by anglers with their rods, hooks, and needs for control and stability, but they require more skill than rafts, are less forgiving among rocks, and need a boat trailer for transport and launch.

Choice of craft for the rivers covered in this book depends on whitewater difficulty, volume of flow, and skill of the boater, plus personal

preferences that are not always logical or even explicable. I, for one, just happen to love canoes. Yet I row my raft whenever that makes the most sense, and I paddle an I-K if I'm backpacking to my put-in destination. Each river summary in this book will address the factors that influence choices of craft.

Information here draws on the author's personal experience, which includes fifty years worth of trips on all the rivers covered in this book plus boating on some 400 different rivers nationwide, and it also draws on reputable guidebooks written by other authors. However,

OPPOSITE: With his decked craft capable of shedding water even when submerged in froth, a kayaker on the White Salmon River of Washington gains momentum to power through the churning hole dead ahead.

Compact to store and easy to carry, inflatable kayaks (I-Ks) are forgiving when glancing off rocks, and they're easier for paddlers to master than hard-shell kayaks or whitewater canoes. Though an expert in both a kayak and a raft, guide Zach Collier riffles down the Wenaha River of Oregon in an I-K because that stream can be reached only by hiking in for miles with his deflated boat in his backpack.

America's Great River Journeys is penned more in the spirit of celebrating these outings and enabling readers to choose their river than in presenting every relevant detail for those wanting an orchestrated excursion. People paddling or rowing in difficult whitewater should consult specific river guides and local maps. Some key sources are listed in the back of this book. Guidebooks and descriptions online will be important for finding some of the put-ins and takeouts for trips featured here.

Difficulty in boating changes dramatically with water level. No single river is the same if the volume has changed. Recommendations here are most relevant for low to medium boatable flows. Difficulty may be greater at high flows. As water rises, rocks sometimes become easier to avoid, but overall hazards generally increase.

Simply choosing the proper season for boating on a particular river is sometimes an adequate strategy for getting a suitable water level. For example, Oregon's Rogue River is almost always boatable at reasonable levels from June through October, and it's likely to be high from April through May. You can count on high threatening flows in Westwater Canyon of the Colorado from May through June, with tamer levels after that. But sometimes it's necessary to know the specific level, especially in the high-water season. This is generally during spring, and continues through early summer in western mountain regions with snowmelt. High water can occur anywhere after rainstorms, which might spike flows suddenly and radically, especially on smaller rivers.

Beware of launching on any rising river or during significant storms. High-water hazards are hypothermia, log entrapment, and long cold swims. Low-water hazards involve foot entrapment in cracks between rocks, plus rocky swims and "wraps" of rock-pinned craft. Learn about these, other dangers, and rescue techniques from reputable sources.

Volume of flow is listed in cubic feet per second (cfs), gauged by the U.S. Geological Survey (USGS). It's risky to generalize, but flows of 200 to 800 cfs are often floatable for canoes and kayaks in rivers with narrow channels, and 800 to 1,000 cfs are often low but doable levels for rafts. Flows of 1,000 to 3,000 cfs are typically a medium level in most river channels. Flows above that constitute a sizable river, with more significant push and force to it. Anything above 5,000 cfs is big, and above 10,000 cfs is truly massive. Flows at these levels unleash a whole different set of hazards and rules of passage where rapids occur. State- or river-specific guidebooks

Stable, durable, and forgiving compared to smaller hard-shell boats, rafts are rowed or paddled. They carry weighty loads of gear and people, tolerate minor collisions with rocks, and accommodate big whitewater. Loaded for a week, Ann Vileisis drifts comfortably down the Grande Ronde River in Oregon.

often include recommended cfs levels for boating, but these usually reflect what experienced paddlers find doable, and do not necessarily represent easy or even safe levels of flow, depending on the boaters' abilities.

Levels can be checked on the internet at USGS sites referenced by state and river. The National Oceanic and Atmospheric Administration (NOAA) River Forecast Center predicts runoff for ten days ahead. Dreamflows.com is excellent for western states and includes judgments for experienced boaters regarding minimum and maximum flows. The locations of relevant gauges for river flows are listed at the start of each river profile in this book.

The flow rate is only one aspect in determining safe and desirable prospects for boating. Difficulty of rapids is another. Rapids are rated Class 1–5 according to the International Scale of River Difficulty by American Whitewater. Ratings cited in this book are largely taken from other guidebooks. In the past few decades, some boaters have downgraded ratings owing to refined equipment and rising skill levels. I tend not to do that, and may report ratings slightly higher than what appear from some sources.

Even Class 1 boating can present challenges to beginning paddlers due to log hazards, swift currents against brushy banks, and treacherous eddy lines on large rivers. So, even for Class 1 rivers, boaters should have proper training and some experience. No one should set out to do any of the trips in this book without prior experience in safe situations and without appropriate skills for the river at hand.

The standard difficulty ratings, as abridged by the BLM, are as follows:

CLASS 1: Small waves, passages clear, no serious obstacles

CLASS 2: Medium-sized regular waves, passages clear, some maneuvering required

CLASS 3: Waves numerous, high, and irregular, rocks, eddies, narrow passages, scouting usually required

CLASS 4: Powerful irregular waves, boiling eddies, dangerous rocks, congested passages, precise maneuvering required, scouting mandatory

CLASS 5: Exceedingly difficult, violent rapids often following each other without interruption, big drops, violent current, scouting mandatory but often difficult

Most of the popular rivers are managed by federal or state agencies in ways that are essential to protecting the rivers' values. Permits are often required to avoid overcrowding; descriptions in this book note if a permit, reserved in advance, is needed. Some of these are in high demand, issued by lottery with application deadlines, and are difficult to obtain. Many permits are available through www.rivers.gov. Others are issued directly by the agency that manages the river. Permits may specify minimum gear requirements, including portable toilets for some rivers and fire pans for campfires. In addition, some states require permits not for a particular trip but for boats, no matter where you go.

Landowners often restrict private property. For access, public land is usually needed. While this can include thin streamfront rights-of-way at bridges or next to roads, public ramps or formal access areas are typically the way to put in or take out for the rivers covered here. Camping should generally be done on public land. Always be considerate, quiet, and low-key, but especially when in sight or earshot of private homes and roads. I never build campfires in those situations.

A curse of globalizing times is that precautions must be taken to not spread invasive species of animals and plants from one stream to another via boating and fishing gear. These exotics pose difficulties and sometimes extinction threats to native river life, and they impose other biological and economic problems. If there's any chance of encountering the exotic quagga mussels, New Zealand mud snails, or other alien species (common especially in low-elevation waters), wash your gear—particularly waders and shoes—thoroughly before going to another stream, especially within two days. Wash mud from footgear and dispose of weed seeds after hiking. Information about and identification of invasive species, by river or state, can be found through internet searches.

Many whitewater guidebooks include introductory tips about technique, safety, and instruction (see source list in the appendix). For the rivers described in this book, beginners would do well to start with Class 1 water if canoeing or kayaking on their own, and Class 2 for rafting. Then work up from there. Even if traveling with a professional outfitter, do not begin with difficult Class 5 water. Many choices are available. Pick what's safe and best for you.

Paddlers thread the needle between sandstone ledges on the Chattooga River in Georgia. Low water presents hazards of rocky swims if paddlers fall out, entrapment of feet within the cracks between shallow rocks, and constrictions where currents can pin boats against exposed boulders.
FOLLOWING SPREAD: A new day breaks with sunrise glowing above the Snake River in Wyoming's Grand Teton National Park.

PART II

THE RIVER
JOURNEYS

NEW ENGLAND

Rivers of New England and the Northeast carve terrain formed by mountain uplifts and then reshaped by continental glaciers. These ancient ice masses scraped landscapes bare and left streams flowing in new patterns across exposed rock strata forming today's rapids and waterfalls. Rivers flow through forests nourished by abundant rain. While some streams rank among the wildest in the East, others transect cultural landscapes dressed with quaint villages—endearing New England to many as the birthplace of the nation—or pass centuries-old industrial towns with brick factories once geared to waterpower.

Most northeastern rivers have been dammed, some of them a dozen times or more. Because of that legacy, free-flowing sections are mostly short, but some remain stunningly beautiful, and a few longer reaches, spared from impoundment, offer extended trips for modern adventurers.

Rivers of Maine include the Allagash and Saint John—the least-developed eastern waterways. Amber seepage from boggy boreal wetlands join the growing flow with alternating rapids and pools, shores thick with black and white spruces, and moose grazing in shallows. Maine's Penobscot cuts a path through Ripogenus Gorge, and New Hampshire's Saco tumbles over gleaming cobbles like a million giant gemstones delivered by glaciers. The Hudson aims down from the wildness of New York's Adirondack Park toward its spacious tidewater valley.

While development here preceded that of other regions, the stature of nature among New Englanders, along with a high level of education and civic involvement, has made the Northeast a hot spot for river restoration. Pollution cleanup, dam removals, and preservation of open space are all notable conservation accomplishments. Streams once repugnant have become magnets of civic pride and business opportunity in an age of river enlightenment that includes canoeing, kayaking, and rafting at its core.

Hearty paddlers in the Northeast squeeze into their wetsuits or drysuits and take advantage of high flows with snowmelt and springtime rain. Summer boating is more carefree, though levels drop in the smaller streams and, with the first radiant warmth, the blackflies, mosquitoes, and no-see-ums hatch, especially in boggy northlands. Bugs wane as the summer wears on. By September and October many rivers drop too low, but those that continue to flow offer irresistible getaways on crisp days when autumn colors in the Northeast are the best anywhere.

SAINT JOHN RIVER | Maine

LENGTH: 114 miles, Baker Lake to Dickey; longer trips possible

WHITEWATER: Class 2, one Class 3 rapid

SEASON: early May to second week of June

GAUGE: Dickey, near the takeout; minimum 1,100 cfs recommended

PERMIT: yes, with fee, no limits, from North Maine Woods

CAMPING: at designated sites

OUTFITTERS: guided trips, rental canoes

HIGHLIGHTS: wildness, long trip, big flow, North Woods expedition

PREVIOUS SPREAD: Rivers of New England and the Northeast wind and cascade through landscapes glaciated during the last ice age and are now shaded by luxuriant forests that transition from deciduous in the south to coniferous in the north. With springtime storms threatening here above the Saint John River, canoeists press onward through dark woodlands and boggy wetlands of Maine's North Woods.

The Saint John River defines eastern wildness in far northern Maine.

In the pantheon of great eastern rivers, the Saint John is the ultimate for length and robust springtime flow through a vast semiwilderness. Virtually no development and only a few road accesses occur through this 114-mile voyage.

Paddlers launch at windswept Baker Lake and soon feel the tug of current that will tumble for days through the closest approximation of the North Woods wilderness that once stretched seamlessly from the Atlantic Ocean to the Great Lakes.

No other eastern river offers such an opportunity to leave civilization behind and enter the realm of a mature river. Amber depths, swift rapids, and shorelines gleaming with melting chunks of ice await while spruce thickets typical of boreal forests farther north darken the shores. The wide river sweeps in long arcs among rolling forested hills with four major tributaries discharging big increments that add markedly to the flow with each day's descent by canoe.

Here's the catch: boaters must slip through the narrow window between ice-out in April and blackflies in June or earlier. Even if one can tolerate those vicious biters, and the thirsty mosquitoes that follow, the water typically drops too low by mid-June. Without rain, the flow declines fifteen percent per day. With rain, the level can stabilize or increase dramatically. To minimize bugs, favor early May; for warmer weather and lower flows, aim for mid- to late May. Every year, of course, is different.

Count on cold rain for at least a day or two. Snow flurries might blow into May. Two modest cabins are available on a first-come, first-served basis, offering shelter from raw wind and cold, though the weather can just as well bring the first intoxicating wafts of springtime. Be prepared

For 114 miles the Saint John River lures paddlers through the North Woods, though the season is short and the challenges of cold weather, variable water level, remote access, and blackflies can be formidable.

with rain gear, winter garb, waterproof gear bags, boating skills, and full-body clothing (light colors to discourage bugs), as well as repellant, headnets, and gloves for the flies.

Even from the freeway in southern Maine, the put-in for this remote destination requires a ten-hour drive. At the far end, roads are passable

but gravel, and fees from a coalition of industrial forest landowners are steep; contact North Maine Woods in advance. But for eastern river aficionados, this rare adventure is worth the cost.

In this big-water experience, most rapids are mild but riverwide—hundreds of yards across with an oceanic feeling. Swift currents and moderate

paddling push canoes 25 miles a day with no problem. Signs mark campsites with fire pits and tables.

One significant drop, Big Rapids, awaits 3 miles above the Dickey Bridge takeout. Large waves, holes at higher flows, and rocks at lower levels challenge less-experienced canoeists. All paddlers should consider the extra burden of boats laden

with camping gear, and the possibility of cold or foul weather. Stay mostly left through this 2-mile choppy descent. Arduous portage at high flows is possible on the left via dirt road.

The trip can be lengthened by starting 18 miles higher at Fifth Saint John Pond, though the drive is worse. And paddlers can go 33 miles farther through pastoral landscapes from Dickey to Fort Kent, and even beyond, for a total of 200 dam-free miles to Grand Falls, New Brunswick.

Halting Dickey-Lincoln Dam—planned near the trip's takeout—became the holy grail of New England conservationists in the late 1970s. The world's largest earthfill dam would have flooded 57 miles of river. Ironically, the hydroelectric site was a compromise rooted in an even worse proposal to flood both the Saint John and Allagash. A vigorous campaign by feisty conservationists halted these threats, though the Saint John still lacks permanent protection that could be afforded by National Wild and Scenic River status—congressional protection from dams for a select group of rivers nationwide (see the epilogue for a description of this system).

College of the Atlantic students and paddler Bob DeForest feel the joy after eddying out at Big Rapids of the Saint John.

A full moon rises over the darkened limbs of spruces and the white trunks of paper birches lining the Saint John River.

ALLAGASH RIVER | Maine

LENGTH: 63 miles, Churchill Dam to Allagash; 98 miles, Telos Lake to Allagash

WHITEWATER: Class 1-2, with one waterfall portage

SEASON: May to September

GAUGE: Allagash

PERMIT: registration required at put-ins, no limits

CAMPING: at designated sites

OUTFITTERS: guided trips, rental canoes

HIGHLIGHTS: lakes, small rapids, North Woods backcountry

The Allagash has long been synonymous with wildland canoe trips in Maine, and paddling here invokes a heritage dating to Henry David Thoreau's sojourns on headwater lakes.

This is a trip for canoeists who like wild rivers and don't mind paddling across lakes as well. Flatwater crossings are linked by languid pools, riffling currents, and Class 2 rapids. Access roads are maintained by industrial timber owners, organized as North Maine Woods, with significant fees.

To minimize lake paddling, start at Churchill Dam, where Class 2 rapids await just below the put-in. Then the riffling sections alternate with three lakes totaling 10 miles. Three or four days later, and 14 miles above the Saint John River, a portage trail bypasses thirty-foot Allagash Falls, followed by more Class 2 rapids.

For a longer trip, put in upstream by driving to Telos Lake, then paddle 35 miles across lakes, including portages at low dams, to Churchill Dam and onward.

The Allagash cannot be run until ice on headwater lakes breaks in April, sending thick floes as battering rams downriver. With some cool rainy weather likely, many paddlers aim for a few weeks in May between ice-out and the scourge of blackflies. Unlike the more difficult Saint John nearby, the Allagash flows adequately all summer, making it far more popular. August and early autumn bring drier conditions, fewer insects, and rockier rapids.

In the 1960s the threat of Rankin Rapids Dam, on the Saint John below the mouth of the Allagash, motivated Senator Edmund Muskie to enlist Stewart Udall, secretary of the interior, to safeguard this favorite northern stream. Proposals for a national recreation area failed to muster state and timber industry support, but a compromise enrolled the Allagash as a state-designated scenic river, and it was later added as the first member of the National Wild and Scenic Rivers System to be administered by a state. The national designation set standards for management of recreation, riverfront logging, and development, though the state's allowance for reconstruction of a dam, replacement of bridges, and encroachment of access roads were contested by Allagash Partners and others, largely without success.

The Allagash River eases northward through its medley of lakes and flowing current.

PENOBSCOT RIVER, WEST AND EAST BRANCHES | Maine

LENGTH: 12 miles of West Branch whitewater; 40 miles on East Branch

WHITEWATER: Class 4–5 on West Branch; Class 2–3 with four portages on East Branch

SEASON: summer and fall

GAUGE: Ripogenus Dam (West Branch), Grindstone (East Branch)

PERMIT: no

CAMPING: no on West Branch, yes on East Branch

OUTFITTERS: guided trips

HIGHLIGHTS: intense whitewater on West Branch, multiday canoeing on East Branch

The West Branch Penobscot churns through the Cribworks with Mount Katahdin towering in the background.

The Penobscot is the third-largest river in New England, after the Connecticut and Saint John. Its basin sprawls across northern Maine with two superlative runs, plus others.

The West Branch at Ripogenus Gorge has the most intense Class 5 whitewater in New England and some of the most challenging in all the East. It ranks with West Virginia's Gauley and Georgia's Chattooga for powerful steep drops.

The put-in, northwest of Millinocket and immediately below Ripogenus Dam, plunges abruptly into a Class 5 torrent called Exterminator. Other Class 4 and 5 challenges follow, including the Cribworks, a maze of impressive waves, holes, rocks, and abrupt pitches.

Except for the most competent paddlers, commercial raft trips are recommended for this dramatic flush of amber North Woods runoff. The rock-walled gorge, massive boulders, lush vegetation, and striking views to Mount Katahdin—5,267 feet on the horizon—make this a memorable trip for anyone who is game to paddle with gusto and get trounced with whitewater in the face. The West Branch is also legendary for landlocked Atlantic salmon through bank fishing at Big Eddy, below the Cribworks.

The East Branch, on the other hand, presents exceptional beauty, wildness, and paddling of an entirely different kind, though not without its challenges. From Grand Lake Matagamon Dam to Grindstone Campground, this medley of swift flow, lively rapids, absolute calm, and four waterfalls is utterly free of roads and development. As a multiday canoe journey with paddling and portaging demands, the East Branch is among the best in eastern America.

The first 8 miles—including the Class 2 Stairstep Rapids—lead to Haskell Rock Pitch, carried on the right, then 2 more miles to Pond Pitch, portaged left, another 1.5 miles to the left shore at Grand Pitch's two-part waterfall, and finally another mile to Hulling Machine, carried on the right. Trails with woodland wonders skirt these drops, and just to see them is worth the portages. Meanwhile, shady campsites enhance this classic North Woods tour. Blackflies, mosquitoes, and no-see-ums can be troublesome until late summer. Moose might be encountered as they wade and graze on aquatic vegetation—keep your distance!

In 2016 President Barack Obama designated much of the area surrounding the East Branch as Katahdin Woods and Waters National Monument—the result of land donations from Burt's Bees founder Roxanne Quimby—now managed by the National Park Service.

Portions of the 91-mile main-stem Penobscot below the East and West Branch confluence at Medway are also boatable. A pleasant Class 1–2 canoe outing navigates wide riffling waters from Mattawamkeag to West Enfield, complete with islands, girthy silver maples, and bald eagles.

Conservationists launched a spirited campaign to protect the Penobscot when faced with plans in 1986 for a West Branch dam at Big Ambejackmockamus Falls ("Big A"), in the rafting section described here. The developer eventually failed to meet the state's Land Use Regulatory Commission requirements.

Additional efforts have been waged for Atlantic salmon, which survive at a fraction of historic numbers but still return to the Penobscot

more than they do to all the other four New England streams having remnant populations. In 2004 a pathbreaking restoration agreement led to the demolition of two fish-impeding main-stem Penobscot dams and improved fish passage at another.

Boaters drawn to this river's stellar qualities might also like the powerful whitewater of Maine's Kennebec Gorge below Moosehead Lake, Dead River's continuous Class 3 turbulence, and the Machias River's overnight canoe route with rapids and small waterfalls much like the East Branch.

OPPOSITE: Author Tim Palmer pulls to the left in the Class 3 runout below Haskell Rock Pitch on the East Branch Penobscot.

A moose wades to graze on underwater vegetation in the East Branch Penobscot.

SACO RIVER | New Hampshire

LENGTH: 4 to 34 miles; 82 miles total

WHITEWATER: Class 1-3

SEASON: April to May; to October for the lower reach

GAUGE: Conway

PERMIT: no

CAMPING: private campgrounds along the upper river; sandbars below Swan's Falls

OUTFITTERS: guided trips; canoe, kayak, and tube rentals

HIGHLIGHTS: rapids, mountain scenery, riparian corridor, easy access

On low flows in June, canoeist Travis Hussey finds the open route through a gallery of glacial cobbles in the Saco River below Conway.

Drift on gentle currents, dodge granite boulders, catch eddies and sweet lines of current notched into bedrock ledges, and appreciate views of the White Mountains' elegant forested summits.

New England offers a lot of intriguing rivers flowing between old dams in this region of early American charm, and the Saco of eastern New Hampshire has easy access, liveries for all manner of craft, campgrounds, and tourist amenities including the restaurant of your choice.

The bustling recreational valley caters to crowds from Boston and other East Coast cities only a few hours away, yet the river—with its rocky corridor and umbrella of riparian forest—is mostly what floaters see from the water. Characteristic of New England, the Saco threads the thin line between culture and nature, and paddling here puts you squarely in the midst of both.

Day trips of variable length begin at fourteen ramps or road-accessible beaches. Rapids range from a Class 3–4 headwaters blizzard in springtime above Bartlett, to gentle flows spiced with Class 2 interludes, to serene windings through one of the finest riparian forests in the Northeast. Camping at shoreline sites along the upper river is discouraged, though busy commercial campgrounds near Conway are available. Below Swan's Falls Dam, gentle water shimmers past thirty sandbars luring boaters ashore to swim, picnic, and pitch a tent for the night.

Liveries and shuttle services make logistics easy, even for the unequipped. With the convenience comes a lot of floating traffic on weekends; it's better to paddle here at other times. Be ready for blackflies in late spring and mosquitoes in summer; carry repellant when canoe camping on the lower section. Take your pick from several reaches of this eminently accessible stream:

- Nancy Brook to Bartlett: This is for experts only on springtime snowmelt.
- Bartlett to Humphrey's Ledge: Nine miles offer Class 2–3 rapids before June.
- Humphrey's Ledge to River Road, North Conway: Four miles flow as Class 2.
- River Road to Highway 302 bridge (Smith-Eastman access): Ten miles flow as Class 2.
- Highway 302 to Weston's Bridge: Seven miles of Class 1–2+ is runnable into summer.
- Swan's Falls Dam (north of Fryeburg) to Hiram, Maine: With 33 miles of Class 1, this lakebed of the ice ages offers quiet winding currents, sandbars for camping, and riparian forests, and is runnable all summer, with intermediate access.

The Saco River Recreation Council maintains accesses and charges modest fees for day use.

From Hiram down, Maine's lower Saco has its appeal, but it is mostly flatwater interspersed with six dams.

Though its beauty qualifies this stream as an outstanding river trip, it's included here principally for its ease of paddling, access, and services. A few other New England favorites for paddling are the Androscoggin and Pemigewasset Rivers in New Hampshire, West and White in Vermont, Deerfield and Farmington in Massachusetts, and Housatonic and Shepaug in Connecticut.

HUDSON RIVER | New York

NEW ENGLAND

LENGTH: 17 miles in Hudson River Gorge; additional day trips below

WHITEWATER: Class 3–4; Class 3 flattening to Class 1 on sections below

SEASON: April to early October; dam-release days from June to early October

GAUGE: North Creek

PERMIT: no

CAMPING: yes, but mostly run as day trips

OUTFITTERS: guided day and multiday trips

HIGHLIGHTS: whitewater gorge, wilderness

A professional guide and his crew confront continuous rapids of the Hudson River Gorge in the Adirondack Mountains.

The Hudson River Gorge was one of the first whitewater runs in the East to be regularly paddled and remains one of the most popular. Come here for the rush of big continuous rapids in a setting of Adirondack wilds with shaded forests where cliffs veer up from shorelines and where ridgetops soar another 1,000 feet. This is principally a kayak and raft run, but expert canoeists appear after the flush of winter snowmelt when the river settles into a rock-studded wilderness just hours from New York City. Any tour of eastern whitewater is not complete without this legendary run.

A legacy of whitewater adventuring goes back to 1957 when the Hudson River Whitewater Derby was started. In 1967 Senator Robert F. Kennedy kayaked the gorge to bring attention to legislation pending for the National Wild and Scenic Rivers Act, and Robert F. Kennedy Jr. took up the Hudson challenge a generation later by working to stop pollution on the lower river and with the creation of Hudson Riverkeeper—predecessor to a worldwide Riverkeeper movement.

This popular commercial and independent trip starts on the Indian River. After 3 miles the foaming tributary spills into the Hudson, which would otherwise be too low for boating by summer.

With Indian River's flush the Hudson boils downward through dozens of drops. Stops include tributary waterfalls, tall jumping rocks, and deep pools where anglers cast for trout. The takeout lies near the community of North River. Guided raft trips are popular beginning on chilled weekends in April, peaking with high flows in mid-May, and continuing through early fall. From late June to early October, the required and rationed flows from the Indian Creek Dam are released on Saturdays, Sundays, Tuesdays, and Thursdays.

Below the gorge, the Hudson riffles peacefully for 6 miles from North River to North Creek, then enters a bedrock maze with Class 2–3 rapids for 8 miles to Riparius—often too low by early summer.

Farther downstream, below the mouth of the Schroon River at Warrensburg, a sedate but splendid Class 1 reach of 13 miles tours islands, wild shores, and green mountains with adequate flows all summer. Boating ends abruptly at the savage churn of fifteen-foot Hadley Falls; take out on the right on a modest access path a few hundred yards above. Below there the middle Hudson is blocked by dams through Albany, and then its tidal Hudson Valley section swells toward New York City.

Though included in Adirondack Park, the upper Hudson was vulnerable to dam proposals in the 1950s until grassroots activists convinced state legislators to block reservoir plans. Later findings by National Park Service staff recommended the upper Hudson for the initial National Wild and Scenic Rivers Act; planner and *Flow East* author John Kauffmann wrote, "Of all eastern rivers it seemed the most logical first choice." But lacking political support, the Hudson was deleted from final drafts of the law.

At sunset the Hudson riffles through a quiet section below the community of North River.

Panoramic southern foothills of the Adirondack Mountains rise with rounded green domes above the Hudson River in its gently flowing reach downstream from Warrensburg.

OPPOSITE: Hadley Falls of the Hudson churns in a vortex that requires a mandatory takeout for all boaters at an access area a few hundred yards upstream from the impassible drop. Below this point, dams block the Hudson, and then downstream from Albany it enters its tidal zone, where the waterway's oceanic width dates to when ice-age glaciers blocked the more northerly Saint Lawrence River's passage to sea and shunted the full runoff of the Great Lakes southward via the Hudson, whose estuary broadens onward to New York City and the Atlantic.

APPALACHIAN MOUNTAINS

South of the glaciated Northeast, the Appalachian Mountains continue for 1,200 miles to Alabama. Hundreds of rivers and thousands of streams splay off the multiridge washboard of the 300-million-year-old range. Whether within the Appalachians or beyond, most great rivers of the East have their sources here in rugged green terrain of temperate climate.

Resistant sandstone creates ledges, rapids, and waterfalls. Leafy rhododendron and azalea conceal many of the banks, and the diversity of trees exceeds that of anywhere else in America. Railroads typically track alongside the larger rivers, though many rail lines have been abandoned and some converted to trails or bikeways, such as along the Potomac, Greenbrier, and Pine Creek.

The Appalachians are the birthplace of recreational river running in America. Exploratory journeys down the Youghiogheny, Cheat, Gauley, and others marked the start of whitewater boating that would eventually grow into a river recreation industry, and whole cultures of whitewater were born and continue to thrive in Ohiopyle, Pennsylvania; Albright, West Virginia; and Bryson City, North Carolina.

One Appalachian river or another lies within a half-day's drive from Boston, New York, Philadelphia, Washington, DC, Richmond, or Atlanta, and so a lot of people can reach these rivers with ease.

Paddlers are often confronted with more rocks than water, demanding "technical" finesse through the Appalachians' signature rock gardens. This is in contrast to big flushing rapids that characterize larger rivers through open channels in many other regions.

Day trips are the norm, but some larger rivers are suited to overnight travel, and a few flow for 100 boatable miles or more through wild, pastoral, and developed landscapes. River travel even through fields and towns has its own element of adventure, and boaters can explore places they've never been and view familiar landscapes from angles they've never seen. On the Delaware, for example, paddlers can launch at the main stem's source and paddle for two weeks uninterrupted by dams the whole way to tide line. South of the Delaware and its adjacent and tempting Susquehanna River Basin, the nearly undammed Potomac flows 200 miles from the heart of Appalachia to the nation's capital.

The Appalachians reach their apex in the South where spectacular waters careen off the east-facing escarpment of the range. Here, springtime flows on a multitude of small streams entice expert kayakers, and the Chattooga ranks among America's finest rivers for extreme whitewater and lush forest beauty.

On the west side of the Appalachians, the Ohio River's headwaters feature peaceful wooded windings, such as the Clarion of northern Pennsylvania, and also some of America's most revered whitewater: the Youghiogheny of Pennsylvania; the Cheat, Gauley, and New of West Virginia; and the Nolichucky, Ocoee, and Nantahala of Tennessee and North Carolina, which tilt from the range's southwestern slopes.

Flowing with snowmelt and springtime rain, Appalachian streams rise as soon as winter looses its grip, prompting hearty paddlers to take to the water. Larger rivers keep flowing through hot summers.

DELAWARE RIVER | Pennsylvania · New York · New Jersey

LENGTH: 5 to 210 miles (tidal mileage extends farther)

WHITEWATER: Class 1-2

SEASON: spring, summer, fall

GAUGE: Hancock, Port Jervis, and others

PERMIT: no

CAMPING: yes, with private land limitations

OUTFITTERS: canoe, kayak, and tube rentals

HIGHLIGHTS: Class 1-2 canoe trips; accessible, easy, long outing; history

PREVIOUS SPREAD: Mist rises from the New River in West Virginia while a summer thunderstorm clears above the gorge at sunset.

At the Delaware Water Gap, the river incises dramatically through Kittatinny Mountain.

The Delaware is the only major main-stem river in the East that remains undammed. Its full 198 miles, from the East and West Branch confluence to tide line in Trenton, plus 10 to 20 scenic miles upstream on the East or West Branches, make for the longest dam-free canoe trip in the Northeast. This handsome river lies within a half-day's drive of 60 million people.

While thousands of houses, dozens of small towns, and a few cities are passed along the way, and while much of the frontage outside the Delaware Water Gap National Recreation Area is private land and none of it is truly wild, the full length of this eastern artery—the fourth-largest river in the greater Appalachian region—provides for an extended canoe voyage. With relatively easy rapids, adequate flows through autumn, many access areas, and few pesky bugs to bite or annoy boaters, this is one of the most carefree long river trips in America.

Delightfully relaxing, the miles, the bends, and the Delaware days blend together in a kaleidoscope of scenery: green hills, mountains, riffles that seldom stall in complete flatwater, a chorus of birdlife, bass fishing, quaint small towns perched above the shores, and a trove of historic landmarks from Zane Grey's home to the site of George Washington's stormy Christmas Eve crossing above Trenton, which turned the tide of the Revolutionary War. Bald eagles perch on snags and eye the shallows for fish throughout.

Recreational use is extremely heavy at times in some reaches. Popular sections at Skinner's Falls and at the national recreation area below Port Jervis are often busy and campgrounds filled. Crowds can be avoided on weekdays and during temperate shoulder seasons.

Along the 75-mile upper river, Hancock to Port Jervis, many cabins and summer homes occupy benches or forested slopes, yet most are screened at least somewhat by trees. Riffles are almost constant, and a few larger Class 2 rapids enliven paddlers with waves above Hankins, below Cochecton at Skinner's Falls where bedrock slabs are run on the right and deserve scouting (on the left), at swift water upstream from Lackawaxen, and elsewhere. Boaters can tie up and stroll into the village of Callicoon for refreshments.

In this upper reach, camping is officially limited to developed campgrounds, rare above Cochecton but more common from there to Port Jervis, and crowded on weekends. Small islands, remote bends, and back channels away from roads and development are occasionally found.

The middle Delaware—47 miles from Port Jervis and downstream through the Delaware Water Gap to Portland—is maintained by the Delaware Water Gap National Recreation Area, with free wooded campsites marked at the water's edge. Most is flatwater except for the minor rapids below the Interstate 80 bridge where the river carves 1,400 feet deep through Kittatinny Mountain.

Below Portland, much of the lower Delaware's 76 miles flow through private land, but wonderfully remote sections beckon at many bends and in secluded channels behind islands. Sloughs and isolated riparian forests appeal from Frenchtown to Stockton. Parkland trails at Bulls Island, across from Lumberville, tour impressive old-growth hardwoods. Historic canals line one or both sides of the river for 30 miles, Easton to Trenton, and create their own buffer of tree-lined open space.

Towns along the lower river are framed in picturesque views from the water while historic

bridges are artfully latticed with iron trusses. Portland, Milford, Frenchtown, and New Hope invite travelers to step ashore, stroll historic districts, and relax in restaurants. The steeples and domes of Easton rise up above the waterfront, and at Trenton the gold-painted New Jersey Capitol gleams above the river's last rapid at tide line. Even there and beyond, the Delaware has green and forested banks and islands.

On this lower section, concrete wing dams jut out from the shores at Lumberville (5 miles above Stockton), New Hope, and Scudder Falls (above Yardley). These three rock and cement causeways extend from either shore toward the center and deserve caution, especially at high flows, as they channel powerful currents through a midriver

OPPOSITE: A busy summer day on the Delaware attracts hundreds of boaters at Skinner's Falls, bordering Pennsylvania and New York. Inexperienced paddlers in rented canoes recover in the pool below the rapid.

Out for an evening after work, fun-loving paddlers enjoy gentle waters of the Delaware below Milford, New Jersey.

The lower Delaware is within a half-day's drive of 60 million people, yet a green riverfront corridor endures for most of its passage. This natural scene lies just below the bustling tourist burg of New Hope, Pennsylvania.

OPPOSITE: Historic Easton rises from the banks of the lower Delaware in Pennsylvania. Even through small towns and a few cities, this eastern artery offers an intriguing cruise for 200 miles.

opening. Below New Hope, the route through the wing dam, at last note, was left-center and then sharply left.

For the satisfying, full journey to tidewater at Trenton, take out below both the Highway 1 bridge and the stadium, at a large public ramp on the left.

Throughout the river's length, scores of access areas and riverfront parks are open to the public. Commercial campgrounds fill on weekends. See the Delaware River Basin's packet of 10 maps for more information.

At Tocks Island, 6 miles above the Delaware Water Gap, a 140-foot dam was proposed in the 1960s, but citizen activists succeeded in stopping the flooding of 37 miles of the Delaware, which were made a river-centric national recreation area instead. And, for the full distance from Hancock to Trenton, most of the Delaware has been designated a National Wild and Scenic River. After heated controversy along the upper reach, local municipalities adopted a plan that excluded significant public acquisition of riverfront open space.

Any number of day trips, weekend outings, or longer expeditions are possible on the Delaware, and its full length offers an expedition unmatched in the East for its length of pleasant dam-free flow.

A historic steel truss bridge
at Frenchtown, New Jersey,
crosses quiet waters of the
lower Delaware while sunlight
begins to dissipate the fog
filling the valley at dawn.

PINE CREEK | Pennsylvania

LENGTH: 5 to 45 miles

WHITEWATER: Class 1–2, with one 2+ rapid

SEASON: spring, 500 cfs minimum

GAUGE: Cedar Run

PERMIT: no

CAMPING: yes

OUTFITTERS: guided trips, canoe and kayak rentals

HIGHLIGHTS: Pennsylvania's Grand Canyon, forests and villages, small rapids

Pine Creek carries the kayak of Ann Vileisis southward through wild terrain and toward the West Branch Susquehanna.

For mostly easy paddling through a green canyon of Appalachian splendor, Pine Creek is ideal. Really a river, this stream showcases the heart of Pennsylvania's northcentral highlands. Known as the "Grand Canyon of Pennsylvania," the 800-foot-deep gorge hides in velvety-green folds of the Allegheny Plateau and runs without roads 17 miles from the Ansonia ramp (Highway 6 west of Wellsboro) to the village of Blackwell. Below there, the lightly traveled but paved Highways 414 and 44 track the river for 40 more miles to the town of Jersey Shore on the West Branch Susquehanna.

Pine Creek is runnable only when the water's up in springtime, best in May. Go earlier if you're game for April's chill, and maybe later on the heels of a rainstorm. Class 2 rapids settle to Class 1 riffles that flatten out the farther you go. The most challenging drop, Owasee, comes 3 miles into the trip below Ansonia. Scout and hug the left shore for the safest route, as it's a long way to road access. Delightful small rapids take you to Blackwell, with wildland campsites along the way.

Many people paddle only the canyon reach, spending a long day or two days, but below Blackwell, Pine Creek continues for another 21 miles to Hamilton Bottom access north of Waterville and even beyond to the West Branch Susquehanna. The rapids downstream from Blackwell are easier, and the road provides multiple accesses at or near the Appalachian villages of Cedar Run, Slate Run, and Cammal. Most have lodging, and campsites are found on state forest shores and islands.

Thanks to a rails-to-trails conversion, a bikeway runs 62 miles from above Ansonia to Jersey Shore—perfect for shuttles. Hiking trails ascend several tributary creeks. Fishing can be good for bass and for native brook trout in cool tributaries.

Pine Creek has created the "Grand Canyon of Pennsylvania" and offers a Class 2 retreat within the deeply forested Appalachian Plateau.

CLARION RIVER | Pennsylvania

LENGTH: 8 to 63 miles

WHITEWATER: Class 1-2

SEASON: spring, summer, fall

GAUGE: Cooksburg

PERMIT: no

CAMPING: yes

OUTFITTERS: canoe, kayak, and tube rentals

HIGHLIGHTS: eastern old-growth forest; long, easy river; runnable all summer

APPALACHIAN MOUNTAINS

The Clarion River meanders with a 63-mile trip that in most years can be done all summer. This beech tree and colorful dame's rocket lie downstream of Hallton.

For the rare combination of an easy five-day trip through semiwild terrain, streamside camping, multiple accesses, and adequate flow through all but drought summers, the Clarion of northwestern Pennsylvania is a great choice. Once tragically polluted with pulp-mill and coal-mining waste, it now runs clear—a remarkable restoration success story in progress.

Paddling begins just below Johnsonburg with access off Highway 219. Gentle rapids aim south in multiple segments to the backwaters of Piney Dam, northeast of the town of Clarion.

Recovering forests green shorelines and hills of the Appalachian Plateau. Clear Creek and Cook Forest State Parks highlight the route. Cook Forest harbors the East's foremost old-growth grove of eastern hemlocks and white pines, seen along trails that are easily reached from the riverfront. The Longfellow Trail, near the ramp at Highway 36, loops through the largest grove.

Favorite sections for easy paddling lie above and below Cook Forest and its liveries that do robust business on summer weekends. Recreational cabins are found in some sections of the Clarion, while others have no development. Coal mining and gas drilling remain problems and threats, but if the Clarion's recovery can be sustained, this river will continue to improve with the passage of time.

Among twenty-seven rivers initially studied for addition to the original National Wild and Scenic Rivers Act, the Clarion was rejected because of pollution, but after cleanup, 52 miles were designated in 1996, and the Western Pennsylvania Conservancy has bought strategic riverfront parcels as open space.

Minor Class 2 rapids spice
the Clarion float near Clear
Creek State Park.

YOUGHIOGHENY RIVER | Pennsylvania · Maryland

LENGTH: 8 miles, plus two other reaches

WHITEWATER: Class 3-4; also with Class 2 and Class 5 sections

SEASON: spring, summer, fall

GAUGE: Ohiopyle State Park

PERMIT: yes for the lower Yough whitewater run

CAMPING: no, day trips only

OUTFITTERS: guided trips, rental rafts; rental canoes on the middle Yough

HIGHLIGHTS: whitewater day trips, waterfall, America's most festive paddling town, an upper run with expert whitewater

The Youghiogheny (pronounced Yock-a-GAY-nee, or "Yock," for short) is the whitewater aficionado's river of dreams. Below the Appalachian town of Ohiopyle, this river offers a steady diet of intricate rocky rapids replete with tight moves, surfing waves, keeper holes, powerful chutes, and complex routing that keeps intermediate and advanced paddlers from ever getting bored.

First come the fast flume and breaking waves of Entrance Rapid. Then the powerful flush of Cucumber. Then one rock-studded rapid after another. The "Ohiopyle Loop" features seven picturesque drops in a 1.2-mile horseshoe bend that comes within a quarter mile of meeting itself, allowing a short carry back to the beginning, where

it can all be run again. It's the closest thing to the paddler's fantasy of a whitewater river that goes around in a circle. Shorelines of the entire 8-mile lower Yough lie within Ohiopyle State Park.

Tightly regulated under park protocols, boaters put in below Ohiopyle Falls with reservations rationed by the half hour. Commercial groups of eighty clients each launch with six people per raft and athletic kayaking guides who coach and rescue their charges at sixteen major rapids. Rental rafts are also available without guides, though previous experience is recommended.

Long a hot spot to kayakers on their learning curve toward advanced status, the Youghiogheny is also the ultimate location for expert whitewater

Guided rafters find the perfect path through Cucumber Rapid.

OPPOSITE: The Youghiogheny River of southwestern Pennsylvania flows through Lower Railroad Rapid while oaks, ashes, and maples turn brilliant in autumn. The Yough was one of the first rivers to attract intensive paddling use.

canoeists, with rapids that offer seemingly endless choices of lines to follow and usually forgiving pools for recovery.

Commercial whitewater rafting had important origins here, with Lance Martin and other outfitters pioneering the use of Army surplus gear in the 1960s and graduating with local innovations through the decades that followed. Once a sleepy Appalachian backwater, Ohiopyle now bustles with boaters, bicyclists, hikers, and crowds who come to see the natural features. Centerpiece to it all, Ohiopyle Falls is one of the East's largest waterfalls in volume of flow. The park also features a busy bicycle trail on an abandoned rail line above the banks—part of a longer Pittsburgh to Washington, DC, bikeway called the Great Allegheny Passage.

Not to be ignored upriver, the middle Yough is a delightful 11-mile Class 2 wildland run through the state park from the town of Confluence to Ohiopyle—an excellent day trip for canoeists working toward intermediate and advanced skills, or for rafters shying from livelier rapids of the lower river.

At the other end of the spectrum, and farther upstream above Youghiogheny Reservoir, the upper Yough—Sang Run to Friendsville, Maryland—is a world-renowned Class 5 paddle-raft or kayak adventure with some of the most challenging technical rapids regularly run in the East. Summer flows for experts or capable guided boaters depend on releases from an upstream hydroelectric dam on Monday, Friday, and Saturday afternoons, mid-June through mid-September.

A classic river of the Appalachians, the Youghiogheny of Pennsylvania rushes over sandstone ledges and rakes banks of lush undergrowth while deciduous forests green mountainsides moistened by early morning fog.

POTOMAC RIVER | West Virginia • Maryland • Virginia

LENGTH: 6 to 177 miles

WHITEWATER: Class 1-2

SEASON: spring, summer, fall

GAUGE: Shepherdstown

PERMIT: no

CAMPING: yes

OUTFITTERS: canoe and kayak rentals

HIGHLIGHTS: gentle canoeing water, long river trips, American history

The Potomac thrashes over the bedrock-studded barrier of Great Falls, Maryland, just upstream from Washington, DC. Canoe trips down the Potomac necessarily take out above here at Riverbend Park on the Virginia side. In volume of flow, this is one of the largest waterfalls in the East, formed by the fall line of erosion-resistant outcrops that occur where rivers drop from the Piedmont Province of Appalachian foothills and meet the Coastal Plain.

A centerpiece river to American heritage, the Potomac winds from West Virginia highlands to tide line in the nation's capital, and it offers some of the choice carefree Class 1 and 2 canoeing in the East. Trips of any length are possible, with up to a full week or more starting at Oldtown, near the South Branch confluence downstream from Cumberland, to the backwater of Great Falls Dam, upstream from Washington, DC.

Paddlers can drift for days with gentle currents, long quiet pools, fast riffles, and occasional Class 2 rapids crosscutting sandstone ledges where Appalachian ridgelines angle dramatically against the river's eastbound route. Remote gravel bars, islands, and wooded benches invite camping, and deep pools tempt swimmers in summer's heat. Four low dams require short portages between Hancock and Harpers Ferry, and a few others have washed out in floods, leaving rocks as obstacles to dodge.

The Cacapon Bends loop in picturesque bowknot patterns upstream of Hagerstown. At Harpers Ferry, centuries-old buildings perch on hillsides with stone walls and with steeples pointing high while summits of Blue Ridge and South Mountains rise 1,000 feet higher. Just below, sandstone outcrops lie awash in Whitehorse Rapids.

Like the Delaware, the Potomac offers a long canoeing trip on easy water with many undeveloped shorelines and occasional small towns, but here boaters encounter several low dams and more vacation homes and cottages.

The final takeout at Riverbend Park on the Virginia side is mandatory, as the six-foot-high Great Falls Dam, just below, is followed by Great Falls itself. This twenty-foot plunge is the East's second-largest waterfall in volume of flow and draws crowds of sightseers from Washington, DC. Below, through the rocky maze of Mather Gorge, the Potomac offers another 8 miles of Class 2 boating to a takeout above Little Falls Dam. Then the lower river eases to tide line at Georgetown and the nation's capital. A widening estuarine Potomac continues 121 miles until fully broadening as the second-largest tributary to Chesapeake Bay.

Source waters of the Potomac's South Branch through Smoke Hole, West Virginia, offer one of the central Appalachians' prime day trips for advanced whitewater canoeists in springtime, as does the North Fork of the South Branch beneath Seneca Rocks' towering cliffs.

The Potomac has been a model of river restoration after sewage was treated and coal-mine acid reduced in headwaters. Construction of sixteen dams proposed by the Army Corps of Engineers was averted in the 1970s. One, on the North Branch below Kitzmiller, Maryland, was built.

This waterway serves as an unofficial "Nation's River" through the capital and with the streamside corridor of the Chesapeake and Ohio Canal protected intact and managed as a bicycle trail by the National Park Service for 185 miles from Washington, DC, to Cumberland, which includes colonial-era towns along the river's path. Connecting as the Great Allegheny Passage, the bike trail continues westward over the Appalachians and down the Casselman, Youghiogheny, and Monongahela Rivers to Pittsburgh—one of America's great long-distance bicycle trails.

Short Hill Mountain rises over the Potomac River while the sun sets at a remote island campsite downstream from Harpers Ferry, West Virginia.

FOLLOWING SPREAD: Separated from the Potomac's long boatable reach that lies above Great Falls, paddlers Jim Palmer, Chris Brown, and Ann Vileisis glide through a perfect summer evening just upstream from Washington, DC.

NEW RIVER | West Virginia

LENGTH: 14 to 42 miles

WHITEWATER: Class 3-5

SEASON: spring, summer, fall

GAUGE: Hinton, Thurmond

PERMIT: no

CAMPING: typically day trips; camping is possible above Thurmond

OUTFITTERS: guided trips

HIGHLIGHTS: high-volume whitewater, Appalachian gorge

In the heart of the New River Gorge, Middle Keeney Rapid sieves through undercut rocks that should be avoided by paddlers.

The New River just happens to be the oldest river in North America and also the biggest whitewater for half the country—a Grand Canyon of the East. Nothing compares to its flow through a forested cleft incised 1,400 feet deep within an ancient plateau.

The river's rank in age and volume of whitewater are intimately connected. The New was in place before the 300-million-year-old Appalachian Mountains arose, and unlike other rivers that were bifurcated as the mountains reared up underneath them—and thus reduced in length and size—the New was large enough to maintain its antecedent path by crosscutting through emerging bedrock. This geologic history is responsible for the volume of flow coming from a vast headwaters sourced far eastward, and also for the rapids—crossing the backbone of Appalachian uplift—that lure boaters to the deep gorge today.

Poised above the New's powerful drops in a raft, paddlers feel the push and inevitable plunge into scouring holes and then the loft onto waves rising roller-coaster high. Sandstone remnants the size of cars and buses have fallen from ancient mountaintops to line the shores and congest the channel. The rapids' thrilling passages split around some rocks and ominously undermine others, eddy into depthless pools, then plunge again. At Keeney Brothers Rapids, three giant stairsteps require paddlers to position and then dig into the foam to avoid undercut rocks left and right.

Commercial guides have run this river virtually every day, spring through fall, since the 1970s, with few serious mishaps but always with respect for whitewater so big that it's found only here and on a few rivers in the West.

whitewater from McCreery (left) or nearby Prince (2 miles upstream on the right) to Thurmond, with a few big waves and holes that canoeists will want to avoid.

The signature trip here is the gorge: a 14-mile lineup of notorious drops from Thurmond to Fayette Station, which is located downstream of the Route 19 bridge—the third highest in the United States.

Normal summer flows range from a rock-studded 1,000 cfs to a channel-bursting 8,000 cfs. Flows of 2,500 to 10,000 cfs are considered good for rafting. The New spikes much higher after torrential summertime thunderstorms that torment West Virginia's mountains, and has risen from 8,000 to 100,000 cfs overnight! Commercial outfitters stop rafting at 34,000 cfs.

Advanced kayakers flock to the gorge, but most rafting is done with commercial companies. Adventures on the Gorge is a full-service resort with expert guides working here and on the nearby Gauley.

Far upstream in North Carolina, the South Fork New River is well suited for Class 2 canoeing. And, joining the New just below Hinton Dam and immediately above the New River section featured here, the Greenbrier River offers an extended canoe trip of 130 miles from Cass to Talcott with Class 2+ rapids in spring and early summer. Larger rapids and a waterfall await below Talcott.

The New River Gorge was designated a national river in 1978, and much of the canyon was acquired as a 53-mile-long preserve managed by the National Park Service for boating, hiking, mountain biking, rock climbing, fishing, and botanizing in diverse habitat. The gorge is one of the East's foremost examples of a landscape that has recovered from a rapacious history of unlimited logging, mining, and railroad construction.

Making it look easy—and certainly fun—river guide Jo-Beth Stamm puts her raft and paddlers where they need to be as she approaches a powerful jet of whitewater in the New River Gorge.

OPPOSITE: The New River Gorge produces the highest-volume whitewater in the East, comparable at times to the Grand Canyon of the Colorado.

The featured section of the New's full 320-mile length lies below Hinton Dam and runs 42 miles to Fayette Station. This can be floated as one piece, but it is typically done as three separate day trips.

Uppermost, from Meadow Creek access below the unrunnable Sandstone Falls to McCreery, 13 miles of big-volume Class 2–3 whitewater is for kayakers or rafters and for canoeists capable of two significant drops, with camping possible. The similar second section is 15 miles of Class 2–3

As the New River's major tributary, the Greenbrier River reflects the vivid emerald green of an Appalachian summer.

GAULEY RIVER | West Virginia

LENGTH: day trips of 12 and 16 miles each

WHITEWATER: Class 5

SEASON: September, October

GAUGE: Belva (below Swiss)

PERMIT: no

CAMPING: no

OUTFITTERS: guided trips

HIGHLIGHTS: one of the most demanding whitewater runs in the country, wild gorge

The Gauley has some of the most demanding whitewater regularly run in America. The National Park Service states that the river's "vigorous rapids, scenic quality, and inaccessibility combine to make the Gauley River one of the premier whitewater rivers in the world."

From the instant rafts embark beneath Summersville Dam's showy rainbow-arching jet of water released in autumn, this trip is a gripping descent through an Appalachian gorge with no road access. Drops have multiple channels, hidden obstacles in undercut rocks, and a constant push that can throw boats into unfriendly paths.

The unusual autumn boating schedule is governed by releases from an Army Corps of Engineers dam, drawn down for winter flood control. Beginning after Labor Day and continuing for six weekends, the Corps releases heavy flows that reach 2,800 cfs exploding in sixty rapids, including multiple Class 5s and many difficult Class 4 drops. Once strictly the province of experts, the river is remarkably now run by 60,000 people a year.

Except for seasoned paddlers in competent teams, people seeking this extraordinary adventure need to go with commercial outfitters. While the 24-mile length of extreme whitewater is long enough to merit an overnight expedition, the upper and lower Gauley are run as separate day trips.

The harder upper Gauley run flows 10 miles from Summersville Dam to Mason's Branch takeout, where a long walk leads to a Park Service shuttle bus on weekends, or 2 miles farther to Wood's Ferry. Five Class 5 rapids have high consequences of error.

The middle and lower Gauley is a 16-mile run with less intense whitewater but still major rapids,

A paddling crew strains to hold its line at Pillow Rock in the Gauley River Gorge. Unlike the typical high-water regime of springtime, autumn is the boating season here on releases from an upstream dam that's drawn down for winter flood control.

taking out at Swiss. Outfitters offer two-day packages with camping nearby. Children under sixteen are wisely not allowed.

Faced with a hydroelectric proposal that would have dewatered the run's uppermost mileage, the Gauley was instead made a national recreation area in 1988 after a spirited campaign for congressional protection.

The Gauley River charges through a wild Appalachian gorge between Summersville Dam and Swiss.

CHATTOOGA RIVER | Georgia • South Carolina • North Carolina

APPALACHIAN MOUNTAINS

LENGTH: 7 to 14 miles

WHITEWATER: Class 2-5

SEASON: spring, summer, fall

GAUGE: Clayton

PERMIT: yes, self registration, no limits

CAMPING: no, but backpack camping along upper reaches

OUTFITTERS: guided trips

HIGHLIGHTS: wild Appalachian gorge, intense technical whitewater

The upper Chattooga in North Carolina is reached only by trail and then by swimming through a bedrock slot incised deep in the Appalachian Mountains.

At the border of Georgia and South Carolina, the Chattooga River ranks as one of the wildest major rivers in the Appalachians and one of the preeminent whitewater rivers of the East and the nation. *Appalachian Whitewater* authors Bob Sehlinger and David Benner wrote that "its excellence rivals any river in this country."

Upper sections are reached by hiking where the river takes shape beneath Whiteside Cliffs, North Carolina. An intriguing narrows above Bull Pen Bridge, west of Highway 107, is reached by trail and by swimming in the crevicelike gap. Downstream, fine trail hiking continues below Burrell's Ford Bridge.

Farther down, Section 2 of the Chattooga begins with access a mile below the Highway 28 bridge and ends at Earl's Ford—7 miles of canoeing with Class 2 and several Class 3 rapids. Even here in relatively mild form, the Chattooga is distinctive as a river of bedrock ledges, which intensify below.

From Earl's Ford to the Highway 76 bridge, Section 3 offers 14 miles of Class 3 rapids with several gnarly Class 4 drops, including the famous Bull Sluice. The modus here is to line up correctly, add forward momentum, and be ready to pivot, paddle, and hang on. This wilderness run would be a phenomenon anywhere else, but at the Chattooga, Section 3 lives in the shadow of what comes next.

Section 4 includes multiple Class 4 rapids and steep Class 5 drops for 8 miles. Vertical plunges, undercut boulders, hidden entry points, and multiple moves to avoid rocks and consuming hydraulics challenge expert paddlers in one of the most technical whitewater runs, culminating with a chain of four Class 5 rapids. The takeout comes after 2 miles of flatwater paddling or getting a tow on Tugaloo Reservoir.

High flows in springtime or after summer downpours create a continuous medley of whitewater with serious consequences of flips or swims. Low water in summer creates boulder gardens requiring complex route finding along with opportunities to eddy out, pause, and select from a cryptic maze of hazards ahead. Steep drops define the term "horizon line" as the route abruptly drops out of sight, leaving boaters looking at treetops.

Section 3 and especially Section 4 are for experts in kayaks and paddle-rafts, and for capable paddlers with professional guides. While flows can drop low in summer and fall, runnable levels last through most of the year. The Chattooga is a must-see for any river aficionado aiming to experience the best and most challenging whitewater in America.

For hikers, 50 miles of trails traverse the gorges. An unrecognized asset is the gorge's status as a botanical wonderland with rare plants, such as the mountain camellia, in lush habitat combining Appalachian splendor with southern latitudes.

Once threatened with further damming, the Chattooga was the first southeastern river included in the National Wild and Scenic Rivers System in 1974 when an explosion in popularity required effective management. The river became a model for coping with issues of safety, access, and popularity from a wide spectrum of the public unaware of the values, fragility, and hazards that a wild river presents.

Among eastern streams, the Chattooga is distinctive not only for the wildness of its roadless gorge and the difficulty of its whitewater, but also because the flows are unaffected by upstream reservoirs, dam releases, and urbanization, which affect all other major Appalachian whitewater runs.

OPPOSITE: A Class 5 drop in Section 4 of the Chattooga sends six rafters on a nosedive. Their pop-up recovery was complete.

Rafting crews from Southeastern River Expeditions pause for a swim and underwater exploration of unusual pothole formations in Section 4 of the Chattooga.

DEEP SOUTH

Flowing to the southeastern coast and Gulf of Mexico, rivers ease across flat lowlands in languorous paths and beneath symphonies of birdsongs. The Coastal Plain lacks whitewater, but remains rich with wildlife, and a host of plant species from both the Appalachians and subtropical latitudes mix with intriguing complexity.

In many of these rivers, amber waters darken in deep black pools while sugary white sand—granulated from quartz bedrock upstream—blankets the shores. Meanwhile palmettos and pines brighten backgrounds even in winter and, together, all these elements make for dazzling tricolored riverfronts of black, white, and green.

As a special delight to Florida paddlers, crystalline springs bubble up from limestone once formed at the bottom of the sea and then uplifted. Drifting by canoe on these gin-clear springflows feels like a balloon voyage over hushed windings of the stream's gentle jungle path. Meanwhile larger rivers spill into miles-wide wetlands of bald cypress and tupelo.

While rivers of the South have been fragmented by channelization, farms, and development, long voyages can still be taken, including the Suwannee from Okefenokee Swamp to the Gulf of Mexico.

River travel on streams such as Florida's Wekiva takes on a characteristic ease with low gradient, warm water, and hot weather, but bugs can range from pesky to overwhelming. Keeping alligators and cottonmouth moccasins in mind, be judicious about swimming and careful when tramping through undergrowth. But a bona fide threat in this region where reptilian lore is regaled is not likely.

In summer, sweltering heat matches steaming humidity, making river time a relief to local paddlers. But for people traveling from elsewhere, winter is the season for river tripping here, especially on Florida's Coastal Plain. When the rest of the country is gripped by January's freeze or frost, daytime temperatures in the Deep South are typically pleasant. Trips here are also fine in springtime, which comes early, and in autumn, which lingers late.

SUWANNEE RIVER | Georgia · Florida

LENGTH: 5 to 235 miles

WHITEWATER: Class 1, several Class 2 rapids, and one Class 2+

SEASON: winter, spring, or fall; hot in summer

GAUGE: White Springs (see also the Suwannee River Water Management District's website)

PERMIT: no; camping permits from Suwannee River Water Management District

CAMPING: yes, but avoid developed land and road access

OUTFITTERS: guided trips, canoe and kayak rentals

HIGHLIGHTS: Okefenokee Swamp; long, gentle flow; wildlife

PREVIOUS SPREAD: With its short and convenient day trip on gentle waters, the Wekiva River sports junglelike vegetation overhanging the stream—nature's sweet interlude near the bustling sprawl of Orlando, Florida.

The Suwannee River begins in Okefenokee Swamp of southern Georgia, where canoeists can literally get lost in a flooded bald cypress forest.

To catch the balmy breezes of springtime, or maybe even a seductively warm spell in the dead of winter, head for the Deep South, and for the essence of that region, there's no better river than the Suwannee. Launch there for the mystique of Okefenokee— perhaps America's most fabled swamp. Downriver, hundreds of bends sweep past live oaks with muscular limbs arcing overhead, glossy-leaved magnolias, groves of pines, thickets of palmettos, and swamps of tupelo. Springs bubble up from the ground, stream sized at birth, so clear and cold that they seem like a gift from cavernous netherlands sent to temper the region's heat. Go for a day or a week or two from the Suwannee's swampland source to endless waters in the Gulf of Mexico.

The Suwannee riverfront presents a lush, recovering tangle of buzzing, chattering, bird-filled habitat. Alligators bask on logs or lay in wait. These dinosaur-era predators intimidate by doing absolutely nothing; only their eyes and nose show, like floating walnut shells, before they disappear underwater with no sound, no splash, no ripple. But you know they're there, teeth and all.

Other wildlife purely delights travelers: great egrets sporting snow-white plumage, pileated woodpeckers drumming on snags, wood ducks whistling when flushed, turtles basking in the sun, and otters peeking up through bristly whiskers. Sixty-five species of semitropical fish swim in the Suwannee, including arrow-sleek longnose gar. Gulf sturgeon reach 200 pounds in one of the species' few reasonably functioning populations; others suffer from dams and channelization. Anglers fish for catfish, bass, and perch. The Suwannee is mostly clean, but pollution threats have grown as industrial dairy farms migrated north from urbanizing counties of southern Florida.

Okefenokee National Wildlife Refuge, north of the Florida state line in Georgia, is a good place to launch a canoe for a short spin or to start a multiweek journey. Canoeists venture into a wonderland of flooded bald cypresses, whose girthy trunks flute out like buttresses in waterlogged ground where you paddle through the forest itself. Campsites—reserved through the U.S. Fish and Wildlife Service—perch on platforms. Alligators will surely be seen, along with marauding raccoons at night; take hard containers for food!

Keeping a compass handy in this homogenous maze lacking topography, landmarks, or even land, one can wind through watery wilderness to their heart's content and then set off downriver. Imperceptible flows start at 120 feet above sea level with gradient rationed lazily downward for 235 miles.

Downstream from the refuge, a 22-mile reach meanders through undeveloped woodlands; nominal campsites can be found on natural levees humped slightly above waterline. Gaining volume a day or two later below Fargo, Georgia, the river suds through the largest rapid in Florida at Big Shoals, 10 miles above the community of White Springs. Ride smaller waves on the left, or portage around the sharp limestone bedrock. Then drift and paddle for days on amber waters that grow silty with high runoff from tributaries, but then clear again as springflows of crystalline water accumulate. The Suwannee is reported to have more springs along its mileage than any other river in the world. These effervesce from underground limestone strata, which also rise above in ornate cliffs of rococo patterns created by water dissolving stone.

Below Branford, on the lower half of the Suwannee, large motorboats appear, and some

paddlers end their trip. But many miles of canoe-able water continue. While the basin has been heavily clearcut, farmed, and developed in places, most shorelines remain shrouded in jungle tangles of vines and tropical fans of palmetto leaves.

Landowners here resisted efforts to recognize the Suwannee's unmistakable southern charm with National Wild and Scenic River designation. However, a state program in the 1980s directed funds from a real estate transfer tax to buy river-front open space. In what evolved as a model of protection, and should have been emulated in other states but was not, the Suwannee River Water Management District acquired 110,000 acres along 205 miles of shoreline.

Throughout the winding course, dozens of parks and boat ramps provide access and allow for trips of any length in spring or fall. Summer is hot and buggy. Mosquitoes and no-see-ums can be annoying at any time; wear a long-sleeved white shirt, cover up, and keep repellant and a headnet handy.

Many southern rivers, including the Black and Edisto in South Carolina, Satilla in Georgia, and Withlacoochee and Saint Marys in Florida, also show the beauty and organic richness of this region, but the Suwannee's swampland source, epic length, and notable saltwater ending are together in a class by themselves.

The wide river reaches sea level at Suwannee—several decades ago a cluster of tumbledown shacks, but now an upscale resort community awaiting the next hurricane's inexorable surge onto the floodplain.

Glassy waters enter the realm of the spotted sea trout and widen into the Gulf of Mexico. On calm days it's easy to skirt islands made wholly of oyster shells. Cormorants and oystercatchers congregate while flocks of pelicans bob like animated white islands. At the Suwannee's end, so perfect is the match and so gentle the intersection of elements that the horizon line evaporates in merging light: the river, the sea, and the sky are all as one.

After winding 235 miles across Georgia and Florida, the Suwannee spills into the placid Gulf of Mexico, offering a rare opportunity to paddle downriver and into the sea.

WEKIVA RIVER | Florida

LENGTH: 1 to 14 miles

WHITEWATER: none, Class 1-

SEASON: all year; best in spring and fall, nice in winter

GAUGE: Sanford (Saint Johns Basin)

PERMIT: no

CAMPING: primitive sites bookable through Wekiwa Springs State Park

OUTFITTERS: canoe and kayak rentals

HIGHLIGHTS: transparent spring water, junglelike shores, birds, alligators

This intimate, glassy smooth, spring-fed, semi-tropical gem bursts with botanical wonders, shorebirds, and wildlife.

Start at Wekiwa (spelled correctly here) Springs State Park just north of Orlando. This prodigious spring, converted to a swimming pool, spills quietly through its outlet as the full-grown source of the Wekiva. A ramp there, with rental canoes, leads paddlers immediately to exotic wetland wonders.

Cabbage palms lean over clear dark waters. Bald cypresses tower overhead, bearded with Spanish moss. Sweet gums, oaks, and other southern hardwoods abound with vines curling to high limbs. On logs, alligators calmly sun themselves, perpetually "smiling" with their upturned mouths—no swimming here! Birdlife includes brilliant little blue herons that comb the shores and shallows, and the elusive limpkin.

In less than a mile, and embayed in a garden of whimsically floating water lilies, Rock Springs Run joins the Wekiva from the left. Paddle up this tempting sidelight through its own artsy Eden. Then continue downstream to Wekiva Island and a marina that's privately owned but open to the public. Excursions can also be started there with a rental canoe.

To return, simply paddle back upriver against the swirled current, though one can also stroke another 10 miles down to Highway 46, or even farther to the Saint Johns River, but the waterway widens lakelike with shacks and development anchored on hammocks and banks.

Avoid weekends and perhaps entire summer months, as the tiny Wekiva gets jammed. But in spring or fall it makes for a return to the real Florida where nature bursts at the seams.

Junglelike shorelines evoke a tropical feel to the Wekiva River.

This miniature river was enrolled in the National Wild and Scenic Rivers System as a specimen of the American semitropics found only in Florida. Across the state's northern expanse, other clear or blackwater rivers include the Econfina, Wacissa, Ichetucknee, and Alexander Springs Creek. Longer trips can be run on these and other streams, but the Wekiva offers uncommon ease of access and delight in its lushness of life.

OPPOSITE: The Wekiva River's gentle and transparent flows welcome canoeists to this semitropical retreat in springtime.

An alligator and turtle family share a log in the Wekiva River.

MIDWEST

Rivers of the Midwest once defined the look of the land around them. Riparian forests grew tall, and the waters drew the eye to their shine and their movement, much as a V formation of geese dominates a wide, open sky. But today much of the region is gridded into cornfields with streams channelized as straight as highways. The Midwest is not known for great river trips, yet two clusters of streams still offer outstanding paddling journeys.

In the Ozarks and related mountains of southcentral Missouri and northern Arkansas, a network of clear streams rise with spring-flows from limestone aquifers to form the Current, Meramec, Eleven Point, Gasconade, Buffalo, and other rivers. Paddling here is a local pastime going back generations. Miles of gentle water sweep beneath overhanging silver maples and sycamores. Fish abound and birds flock to the edges. Boating feels carefree in steady flows, and white or tan limestone gravel bars beg for camping.

Other great midwestern trips lie northward in Michigan, Wisconsin, and Minnesota. In northern Wisconsin whitewater is found on the Wolf, Brule, and Peshtigo. The Upper Peninsula of Michigan features a lineup of steep-gradient streams dropping to Lake Superior. Minnesota boasts the upper Mississippi's boggy wind-ings. For a long trip, the Namekagon of Wisconsin flows into the Saint Croix, together offering a week or more of good paddling.

Canoeing in these regions does not generally require advanced skills, and so many of the rivers are great for beginners and serve families, scouts, youth groups, and anglers.

With steady springflows at southern latitudes, the Ozark riv-ers can be paddled year-round. April and May are delightful when blossoms unfurl. Summer is hot and humid, and weekends at popu-lar rivers become jammed with floaters. On larger streams, such as the Current, good flows continue in autumn after the crowds have gone home. On the northern rivers, spring comes late and bugs can be annoying through early summer, while late summer and autumn offer pleasant relief.

BUFFALO RIVER | Arkansas

LENGTH: 8 to 122 miles

WHITEWATER: Class 1-2, Steel Creek to Kyles Landing, then Class 1 to the mouth

SEASON: spring on the upper river to Pruitt, plus summer and fall for the lower river

GAUGE: Ponca (upper river), Hasty (middle river), and others

PERMIT: no

CAMPING: yes

OUTFITTERS: canoe, kayak, and tube rentals

HIGHLIGHTS: long Class 1-2 canoeing, undeveloped wooded shores, limestone cliffs

PREVIOUS SPREAD: The Namekagon River of Wisconsin riffles with gentle flows and shaded shores typical of the Midwest's finer rivers in the northern states and in the Ozark Mountains and their nearby terrain in Missouri and Arkansas.

Headwaters of the Buffalo River make for great paddling in springtime.

With sources in the Boston Mountains of northwestern Arkansas, the Buffalo is excellent for overnight and extended canoe expeditions with its 145-mile length, publicly owned as a National River and managed by the National Park Service. This re-wilded corridor enhances a region otherwise blanketed with private land, farms, and rural development.

At medium and low flows, intimate clear waters riffle with small rapids and grow to a mature river in bends brushing 500-foot limestone bluffs. Water from caves, sinkholes, tributary waterfalls, and springs tint the river a milky green emanating from karst topography. Towns, houses, and farms are absent the whole way to the White River at Buffalo City. Weekend canoe traffic is heavy on upper and middle reaches.

Undeveloped campsites await on spacious tan gravel bars. Developed campgrounds and access areas appear at intervals where local roads wind down to the river or cross at 5- to 20-mile intervals. Drinking water can be resupplied at some of these.

In transitional territory between east and west, as well as north and south, the Buffalo corridor is a mixing zone of plants and birds. Swallows dart at dusk, ospreys perch on treetop snags, great blue herons wade the shallows, and kingfishers rattle their call from one bank to the other. Turtles can be seen swimming in clear depths beneath the canoe. Forty-one species of snakes are native to Arkansas—many of them here, though rarely seen—and an occasional cottonmouth might lurk downriver near the White. An impressive fifty-nine species of fish thrive in the Buffalo; at times schools of minnows cloud the shallows. While drifting or from shore, anglers cast for

smallmouth bass, largemouth bass, spotted bass, catfish, and panfish.

Trails finger out from some recreation sites, but beware of poison ivy, which grows almost everywhere, and of ticks at grassy edges. Floaters must also be conscious of high flows and radically spiking crests that come unexpectedly with torrential rainstorms. Anyone going to the mouth must turn upriver when entering the White River and paddle an easy mile to Buffalo City's ramp.

The upper Buffalo is best and most intimate for 30 miles from Steel Creek to Carver. Another highlight, starting 15 miles farther down, Woolum to Maumee features islands, gravel bars, cottonwood groves, and scenic bluffs for 30 miles. Midway downriver, near the Highway 65 bridge, Gilbert Dam was proposed in the 1960s, prompting citizens to campaign for the National River designation.

Paddling is possible even in winter with a warm and storm-free forecast. Springtime boating on the entire river is superb, especially after high muddy flows subside. Runoff continues in late summer and autumn on middle and lower reaches.

Limestone cliffs of Big Bluff stand tall above the Buffalo River.

CURRENT RIVER | Missouri

LENGTH: 6 to 112 miles

WHITEWATER: Class 1

SEASON: spring, summer, fall

GAUGE: Akers (upper), Van Buren (lower)

PERMIT: no

CAMPING: yes

OUTFITTERS: rental canoes, kayaks, rafts, and tubes

HIGHLIGHTS: springs, long Class 1 trip, clear water, birds

A single springflow at Pulltite forms this impressive outlet stream, bubbling past sycamores and silver maples to join the Current River. The Ozark Mountains boast one of the highest concentrations of spring-water discharges in America.

Flowing near the geographic center of the United States, the Current is arguably the finest Class 1 extended river journey in the nation. For 108 miles virtually all the frontage is public land, administered by the National Park Service as Ozark National Scenic Riverways. It is ideal for a vacation of a week or two through a linear national park complete with ramps and campsites—both developed and natural on countless bars of white gravel. Along with the Buffalo National River, this stream in public owner-ship is unequaled among gently flowing, accessible, and easily paddled rivers in America.

Within this Ozark Mountain region, lime-stone bedrock and karst topography spawn the greatest concentration of freshwater springs in America. Chilled from their depth underground, they pour into the river through rivulets and also as fully formed streams large enough for canoe-ing. Paths lead to some of the bubbling sources. Dissolving limestone tints crystalline water blue-green in deep pools. Plentiful wildlife includes turtles, beavers, minks, and otters. Birding is lively, and bass fishing popular.

With timeless appeal, the Current has drawn floaters for generations. To avoid crowds, noise, and competition for campsites, go in spring, fall, or on summer weekdays. Sudden flooding after summer downpours poses one of few hazards; if storms threaten or dark clouds gather upstream, select campsites with options for retreating to higher ground.

Pleasant canoeing begins near the upper end of the designated National Riverways below Montauk State Park, southwest of Salem. With dependable summer flows 25 miles downstream, paddlers can launch from Pulltite access for a com-pelling 62-mile trip to Van Buren.

Just downstream, a path leads to Pulltite Spring; other impressive discharges include Round Spring, 10 miles farther, and Blue Spring, which bubbles up near riverside in another 25 miles. The town of Van Buren has a bustling takeout, but the National Riverway continues for another 20 miles of slow water to Gooseneck access upstream from Doniphan. Motorboaters ply this lower section more than above, deterring some canoeists.

The Current's major tributary, Jacks Fork, is also part of the National Riverways. With springtime flows, its slender upper reach enchants for 18 miles from Highway 17 to Alley Spring, followed by 15 more miles to the Current River, canoeable until levels drop in summer.

A 108-mile corridor of the Current River and its Jacks Fork are managed by the National Park Service as the Ozark National Scenic Riverways—a national park specializing in canoe trips. Ann Vileisis takes a break from paddling between early morning thunderstorms.

FOLLOWING SPREAD: The Current River grows with accumulating runoff as it crosses southern Missouri. Cold springflows chill the river and cause hot humid air directly above to condense and create pockets of steamy fog even in midday.

NAMEKAGON AND SAINT CROIX RIVERS | Wisconsin • Minnesota

LENGTH: 6 to 176 miles

WHITEWATER: Class 1-2

SEASON: spring, summer, fall

GAUGE: Leonards (Namekagon headwaters), Danbury (Saint Croix River)

PERMIT: no

CAMPING: yes

OUTFITTERS: canoe, kayak, and tube rentals

HIGHLIGHTS: long trip, Class 1-2 canoeing, camping

The Namekagon River of northern Wisconsin begins with intimate twists through boggy wetlands and grows to a riffling watercourse shaded by maples and maturing white pines. One hundred miles of paddling down this river to its confluence with the Saint Croix is interrupted by only two small dams.

The Namekagon may be the upper Midwest's best extended trip through semiwild country with campsites and no impassable rapids. A superb expedition continues down the Saint Croix River to Highway 70 near Grantsburg, Wisconsin, or beyond. This is an outing for canoeists with camping gear and a week or more to drift on carefree northern waters. Two small dams on the upper Namekagon must be portaged.

For the full experience, put in at headwaters just below the low dam backing up Lake Namekagon at the Highway 211 bridge east of Cable, Wisconsin. Gentle flows through wetlands and muskeg alternate with quick Class 1 and 2 rapids tightly shaded by alders, willows, spruce, cedar, and statuesque eastern white pines. Though roads, villages, and farms encroach nearby, most of the passage is insulated by a thin but significant riparian border that lends a northern sense of wetland wildness. Small campsites can be found where banks occasionally rise above soggy terrain. One low bridge requires a canoe drag, and pools are backed up by disintegrating dams above Seeley and at Phipps—both runnable as Class 2 rapids. In dry years this reach should be done before water levels bottom out. At mile 22 Hayward Dam backs up flatwater for 3 miles, with a portage on the left.

Below Hayward Dam, and runnable all year, a 30-mile section of semiwild river resumes to Trego, Wisconsin, where a 6-mile backwater ends with another low dam, portaged on the right. Then the Namekagon continues with grace and charm for

30 miles to the Saint Croix. No development clutters the river's path through wild, wooded floodplains.

Below the Namekagon confluence, the broader Saint Croix riffles southward for another 42 miles to the Highway 70 bridge west of Grantsburg. Currents ease among hundreds of islands and through lowlands once accommodating a braided sea of ice-age runoff, now thick with silver maples rooted in Pleistocene river channels. Highlighting this reach, a western slough passes the mouth of the Kettle River with easy Class 2 rapids and secluded campsites—enticing except at low flows. Below Highway 70, another 33 miles with wider and quieter water leads to Lions Park upstream from Saint Croix Falls and its dam, which cannot sensibly be portaged.

This lengthy trip is good all summer and fall but most pleasant after the bugs fade, though mosquitoes may linger until frost, especially along the Saint Croix. Bald eagles soar overhead. Anglers fish for trout in the upper Namekagon and bass below.

As part of the two rivers' designation in the Wild and Scenic Rivers System, the National Park Service marks and maintains campsites every 5 miles or so through much of this trip's length.

Among other regional draws are the lower Wisconsin River, sweeping past spacious sandbars that make hospitable campsites along 81 miles leading to the Mississippi. Scenic paddling is also found for 20 miles on the Flambeau's North Fork, including Class 2 rapids, while 27 miles of the South Fork are runnable with portage of Little Falls, 4 miles up from the North Fork confluence.

OPPOSITE: A trip on the Namekagon continues down the Saint Croix River at the border of Wisconsin and Minnesota. Together the two streams offer an extended trip of a week or more. Here the Saint Croix mirrors white pines on islands near the mouth of the Kettle River.

The Saint Croix appeals to paddlers and anglers in its riffling waters not far from Minneapolis-Saint Paul, Minnesota.

GREAT PLAINS

From Montana to Texas, thirty major streams cross the Great Plains, which is like a continental desktop tilted gently east toward the Mississippi. Streams everywhere erode on the outsides of bends and then redeposit silt on the slow-moving insides of bends, but here on the plains that process is especially evident in eroded cutbanks and alternating sandbars. Riverfronts are the only places wet enough for trees to grow, and so cottonwood clusters buffer the waterways and dress them in a charm otherwise lacking through long windings that repeat with little change.

The flatness, muddy water, and monotony of rivers on the Great Plains don't appeal to some boaters, and smaller rivers are crossed by barbed wire fences for cattle while diversions suck out vital runoff for irrigation. But where a semblance of America's original grasslands can be found, the prairie rivers are magnificent in their gliding flow, cottonwood corridors, and big-sky empty spaces.

At the top of this list, the Missouri River exits Rocky Mountain terrain and flows free across the northern plains for 150 miles—a paddler's route to the past of a region that Lewis and Clark praised above all others for its buffalo, elk, deer, beavers, wolves, and waterfowl. Cattle thoroughly claim today's Missouri River corridor, but southward, along the Little Missouri River in Theodore Roosevelt National Park, buffalo once again graze, and the past can be imagined.

Another highlight, the Yellowstone begins in Wyoming, nourishes America's first national park, then follows a marathon route across Montana's plains. Also seminatural, the Niobrara wends through Nebraska's Sandhills of windblown soil that sprouted luxurious grass after the continental glaciers receded.

Wintery weather persists through springtime on the Plains, so river travel is best in summer, when afternoons are hot but windy, and in early autumn as the cottonwoods turn golden.

NIOBRARA RIVER | Nebraska

LENGTH: 7 to 150 miles

WHITEWATER: Class 1-2, plus several portages

SEASON: summer, fall

GAUGE: Sparks (below Valentine)

PERMIT: no, but nominal fee for the launch at Fort Niobrara National Wildlife Refuge

CAMPING: yes, but with limitations of private land and the wildlife refuge

OUTFITTERS: canoe, kayak, and tube rentals

HIGHLIGHTS: unique float through the Sandhills, rare clear-water river

PREVIOUS SPREAD: Riffling near Springdale, the Yellowstone curves across the Great Plains of Montana.

The Niobrara River flows through the rolling Sandhills and across the width of Nebraska. Here, east of Valentine, a dam was proposed but halted when the fine canoeing reach was designated in the National Wild and Scenic Rivers System.

The Niobrara offers a special opportunity to canoe through the Sandhills of Nebraska—a distinctive area of the Great Plains with rolling terrain and freshwater springs nourishing this nearly undeveloped river.

The popular paddling reach extends 22 miles from the Fort Niobrara National Wildlife Refuge launch at Cornell Bridge (downstream from Valentine), with additional accesses. Gentle riffles suit beginners except for Rocky Ford Rapid at the takeout. With fewer floaters, 8 more miles continue below Rocky Ford, including a Class 2–3 rapid, and end at a falls above Norden Bridge; portage left and take out below the bridge with permission from the Niobrara Valley Preserve. The wildlife refuge bans alcohol, so the first 9 miles from Cornell Bridge to Berry Bridge remain a quiet, pleasant trip. From Berry Bridge to Rocky Ford, party boaters might be encountered on summer weekends.

While day trips below Valentine are the big draw, a long and seldom paddled reach above there offers a special window to this region. Its rough edges are not for everyone, but from Lions Bridge, south of Gordon, a narrow channel soon widens with ample groundwater discharges even in summer of most years. Virtually no development and only a few bridge crossings occur in this remote prairie paradise for 100 miles to Valentine. Several state wildlife management area parcels border the river, but most land is private, and many barbed wire fences cross the current (twenty at last count!). Though most are not irksome, these demand constant caution and care to sneak under or drag boats around. It's also possible to harmlessly slip over sagging barbed wire when flows are adequate.

Roughly 50 miles downstream from Lions Bridge, and south of Cody, the river narrows from two hundred feet to fifty feet and then funnels over an unrunnable waterfall and directly into a channel that narrows to an astonishing one foot wide! At this extraordinary geologic feature, the entire river jets through a cavernous undercut passage in sandstone. Stop well above this turbulence and portage the unique impasse.

Below the Highway 20 bridge (south of Valentine), and below a railroad bridge that follows, boaters must take out at Borman Bridge access on the south bank. Below there, and extending to the fifteen-foot-tall Cornell Dam, the river is closed to public use—at least until the dam might someday be removed. Boating resumes below the dam at Cornell Bridge access.

The Niobrara below Valentine is one of only two rivers on the Great Plains protected in the National Wild and Scenic Rivers System. Designation banned the planned Norden Dam, which would have permanently flooded more agricultural land than it would have irrigated.

MISSOURI RIVER | Montana

LENGTH: 42 to 149 miles

WHITEWATER: Class 1, with wind and large-volume flows

SEASON: summer, fall

GAUGE: Fort Benton

PERMIT: BLM registration at put-in, no limits

CAMPING: yes

OUTFITTERS: guided trips, canoe and kayak rentals

HIGHLIGHTS: Lewis and Clark route, Class 1 overnight trip, undeveloped prairie river

The 2,540-mile-long Missouri is the longest river in the United States, and its passage through north-central Montana was one of the crucial routes during western expansion—a watery highway from the Midwest to the Rocky Mountains serving explorers, trappers, and settlers. Undeveloped shorelines and historic sites make this northern Montana section of the "Big Muddy" one of the top seminatural rivers across the Great Plains. Scattered cottonwood groves shade campsites and thicken along the lower half of the route. Though these are wide, windy waters, the lack of rapids makes this run suitable for cautious beginners and competent family groups.

From Fort Benton to Coal Banks Landing, 42 miles curve through private land, hayfields, and low hills. The next 47 miles to Judith Landing become wilder with shortgrass prairie. In the upper part of this section, white sandstone cliffs rise from the shores. This section also sees the most use. Below Judith Landing, unmarred mileage cuts through the Missouri Breaks—rolling uplands incised by ravines in a maze of sculpted badlands. At Cow Island Landing, 126 miles below Fort Benton, terrain flattens somewhat and ranches reappear. A Bureau of Land Management (BLM) campground at Robinson Bridge, 149 miles below Fort Benton, is the last takeout before the 134-mile-long Fort Peck Reservoir.

Midspring through midfall, the Missouri sees 6,000 canoeists a year. Trips of one to ten days lack major rapids, but headwinds blow across the wide waterway, and gusts can create sudden safety hazards or halt downstream progress. The silty water is difficult to filter; drinking supplies should be carried. Mosquitoes can be overbearing early in summer, and rattlesnakes and ticks deserve a

Broad, windy waters of the Missouri flow from the foothills of the Rockies and cross the Great Plains on their way to the Mississippi.

cautious eye when hiking. Partial segments of the trip are possible between five access areas, but the shuttles are all long.

Lewis and Clark navigated here in 1804, and their journals colorfully referenced nine camp-sites and an abundance of buffalo, birds, and other wildlife. Floating today lets us imagine what they saw. Bighorn sheep and elk might be spotted below Judith Landing. Prairie dog towns and tunnel complexes remain a magnet for associated predators and coinhabitants. The river is home to forty-nine fish species and supports the largest of only six remaining populations of paddlefish, up to 140 pounds.

The Missouri was designated a National Wild and Scenic River in 1976, banning a dam once proposed. This reach is the only one that remains somewhat like it was when Lewis and Clark explored; however, changes have been profound. Riverfront cottonwoods were decimated by fire-wood cutting for steamboats, which each burned thirty cords of wood per day, and then by cattle, which ate and trampled seedlings. Recent efforts seek to control livestock and lessen their harm to prairie grasses, trees, and waterways.

Below sprawling Fort Peck Reservoir, another 185 miles of the Missouri drift undammed past low bluffs. Highway 2, farms, and ranchland are never far away, but this reach sees few paddlers and offers another prairie canoe journey.

The famed white cliffs section of the Missouri below Coal Banks Landing is a paddler's favorite reach. For 149 miles this broad, muddy, windy watercourse traverses broken terrain of the Great Plains and still resembles the path that Lewis and Clark traveled.

YELLOWSTONE RIVER | Montana

GREAT PLAINS

LENGTH: 6 to 527 miles

WHITEWATER: Class 2 in large volume from the Carbella access down; a short Class 2-3 section from Gardiner to Carbella lies above

SEASON: summer

GAUGE: Livingston and others

PERMIT: no

CAMPING: yes

OUTFITTERS: guided trips for the uppermost section; guided fishing trips, Carbella to Big Timber

HIGHLIGHTS: America's longest Class 2 canoe expedition outside Alaska, Rocky Mountain views in upper sections, Great Plains tour, birds, fishing

A driftboat and its oarsman approach one of the Yellowstone's many wave-graced rapids downstream from Livingston. Trout anglers fish the river from its upper reaches to Big Timber and even as far as Billings.

FOLLOWING SPREAD: Sunrise illuminates the Yellowstone River and its corridor of Fremont cottonwoods near Springdale. The length of this river displays one of the longest riparian cottonwood corridors in the West and is critical to many wildlife species.

The 670-mile-long Yellowstone begins in one of the wildest enclaves of the forty-eight contiguous states, plunges over one of the West's most impressive waterfalls, loops through the bison-grazed wetlands of Hayden Valley, and after 130 miles leaves Yellowstone National Park and later crosses the Great Plains. Hearty flows riffle summerlong. At its mouth, the Yellowstone averages 13,000 cfs while the longer Missouri carries only 11,000 cfs.

Among the ten major rivers flowing from the Rockies, only the Yellowstone and Salmon remain unblocked by storage reservoirs. Though often cited as the longest dam-free river in the United States outside Alaska, the Yellowstone is not completely dam-free; six low-head diversion structures include one channel-wide blockage that requires portage by canoeists. The others are variably runnable or not depending on boaters' skills and the approach taken at each dam. Whitewater does not exceed Class 2 from Carbella down, but this section includes hundreds of rapids with breaking waves or holes that paddlers in loaded canoes will want to avoid, often by angling left or right after entering the upper tongue of the rapid.

Though ranches, railroads, an interstate highway, irrigation works, and houses are all part of the mix, this river offers enticing views throughout, swift water, and mature cottonwood forests. As a large, healthy, free-flowing river, this one still creates new channels, carves banks, creates logjams, and nourishes habitat for a wealth of fish, birds, and other wildlife the way other arterial rivers used to do when their natural processes were intact. I've seen more bald eagles on this river than almost anywhere else.

At intervals of 10 miles or so, accesses connect to highways that parallel both banks, though the roads are unobtrusive from the water. Trip possibilities range from a half day to a month, with resupply possible by walking a mile or so into several prairie towns. The upper reaches offer a rare tour of Rocky Mountain scenery from a canoeable river, and below Livingston the Yellowstone becomes the premier natural river of the Plains. Consider these four sections:

- Gardiner to Carbella access: Below Gardiner, Class 2+ whitewater runs 4 miles; 9 miles farther, Yankee Jim Canyon, with Class 3 turbulence, is suited for rafts and kayaks.
- Carbella to Livingston: Starting at the Carbella ramp a few miles above the Highway 89 bridge, gradient eases to Class 2 for 47 miles through Paradise Valley, passing ranches and the abrupt rise of the Absaroka Mountains to the east and Gallatin Range to the west—views unfortunately now marred by trophy homes scattered on banks, slopes, and ridgelines. Here is some of America's optimum fishing for brown and rainbow trout.
- Livingston to Billings: This stretch includes 132 miles of swift Class 1 with Class 2 wave trains, mountain views, islands, yellow rock bluffs, cottonwoods, and ranches.
- Billings to the Missouri River in North Dakota: This section is 351 miles. At Billings, a river that is still wonderfully scenic passes massive oil and gas refineries, though just below them it resumes natural appeal as a stream linking the mountains with the plains. Cattle, hayfields, road crossings, a railroad, and Interstate 94 all occupy this corridor, but boaters see few of the vacation homes or anglers in driftboats that are common on the

upper reach. Long sections—especially below Glendive where the interstate leaves the corridor—have a surprisingly wild feel with wide, gentle flows, Canada geese honking in multitudes, white pelicans in elegant flight, and not a person to be seen for miles and even days. Cottonwood forests are magnificent, though badly infested by exotic Russian olive trees. Forty-five species of fish include rare pallid and shovelnose sturgeons, as well as anglers' favorites: bass, walleye, and catfish.

All six of the Yellowstone's low-head diversion dams appear from Billings to Intake, which is 17 miles downstream from Glendive. First, Huntley Diversion Dam blocks the right side 14 miles below Billings; stay left of the island for open passage. Waco appears in another 36 miles; again stay left of the island for open water. Rancher Dam comes in another 36 miles and below the Bighorn River; drag or lift over the low structure on the extreme left. Myers is in another 15 miles; stay far left for a Class 2 drop over the dam. Forsyth rises in another 41 miles; go extreme right for a steep three-foot drop next to the southern bank. In another 167 miles Intake Diversion Dam extends riverwide; stop and portage 200 feet on the right. All dams pose potential dangers and may require portage if the proper approach is not taken. Make judgments based on conditions at the time.

Irrigation systems developed in Montana's early days of settlement shunt flows into canals at the diversion dams, and many pumps divert water. Intake Dam blocks migration of endangered pallid sturgeon, which grow to five feet long. Only 125 remain in the upper Missouri basin, and the local population has not reproduced in the wild since dam construction a century ago. At this writing, the Army Corps of Engineers plans to replace the current rock-and-rapid structure with a solid concrete dam costing $59 million, though the planned fish-passage facilities are not known to work for

sturgeon. American Rivers and other groups support dam removal with provisions for pumping irrigation water into canals. Elimination of this minor dam would open 167 miles to spawning sturgeon and other fish and free the Yellowstone of its only full-width dam.

In 1972, a coal-mining boom threatened the Yellowstone with a 31-mile impoundment plotted for Paradise Valley. Related threats of diversions led to a state reservation of instream flows that preclude large withdrawals for energy development. The Yellowstone is America's only example of setting aside substantial flows in a large river for fish, wildlife, and natural hydrologic functions that maintain a healthy riverbed. More recent problems with riprap (rock armoring) along scenic windings of Paradise Valley and below have multiplied, and oil spills have reoccurred from lower-river pipelines that broke in 2011, 2015, and other times.

Many Yellowstone paddlers prefer the one- to three-day trip with iconic mountain views upstream of Livingston, but excellent canoeing water runs from Carbella to the Missouri River—a nearly dam-free expedition of 527 miles. I did this river in September as a twenty-day trip, but foul autumn weather required three layover days.

For a megatrip by canoe, this is unconditionally the place to go, though it's the most enigmatic river in this book. Through long sections, sometimes lasting days, I saw no other boats or people, though the railroad and other intrusions are seldom far off. It's a semiwild, semicivilized river with the features of a great wilderness expedition, but also with opportunities for exit, cell-phone use, and resupply at small towns. The full Yellowstone is an epic journey, incomparable in scale, taking paddlers away for hundreds of miles on a truly great American river journey.

PREVIOUS SPREAD: Spectacularly white, with black wings contrasting in flight, pelicans flock on many gravel bars of the middle and lower Yellowstone (top left). A herd of mule deer gathers along the Yellowstone at daybreak. Both mule and white-tailed deer thrive along the river's riparian corridor (bottom left). Rugged bluffs rise from the Yellowstone's banks upstream from Terry and at many sites extending from the Rocky Mountains and across the Great Plains to the river's mouth (right).

An autumn rainstorm clears on the lower Yellowstone—a classic river of the Great Plains here above Sidney.

ROCKY MOUNTAINS

For those in the know, the phrase "best river trips" conjures up visions of the Rocky Mountains, and especially the rivers of Idaho.

The Rockies run from New Mexico northward, and ten great rivers in this extended uplift of the interior West radiate like crooked spokes in a wheel: clockwise from the north are the Missouri, Yellowstone, Platte, Arkansas, Rio Grande, Colorado, Green, Snake, Salmon, and Columbia. Hundreds of headwater tributaries drain from snowfields, wildflower meadows, and forests of aspens and conifers. Lower canyons carve multiple layers of sandstone, granite, and lava. Clear waters are habitat to trout and the source of drinking water throughout the West.

The northern Rockies offer several multiday glamour trips of the West. Both short outings and extended ones deliver the joy of floating on crystal waters through wild rugged country. The Salmon, Middle Fork Salmon, and more northerly Selway are highlights of this region. Starting at the Canadian border, the North Fork of the Flathead is a superb canoeing stream. The Snake in Wyoming offers the Rockies' most iconic river view as it winds in front of the Teton Range. Far downstream, the same river pummels through one of the deepest canyons in North America. In Colorado, the Arkansas offers some of the best whitewater in the West.

Snow squalls can unpredictably strike many mountain streams through April or even later, so summer is the time to be on rivers here, and autumn boating continues until the heavy frosts of October.

ARKANSAS RIVER | Colorado

LENGTH: 7 to 100 miles, mostly run as day trips

WHITEWATER: Class 3-5

SEASON: June to August 15, when irrigation reduces the flow

GAUGE: Nathrop, Parkdale

PERMIT: no

CAMPING: in campgrounds; nondeveloped camping at a few sites

OUTFITTERS: guided trips, rental rafts and kayaks

HIGHLIGHTS: intense rapids, geology, whitewater community, recreational amenities

PREVIOUS SPREAD: Rivers of the Rockies plunge from highcountry to canyons, valleys, and deserts below. Here at the mouth of Sheep Creek, the Salmon River carves its passage through the mountains of central Idaho.

Class 3, 4, and 5 rapids called The Numbers challenge rafters and kayakers on the Arkansas River upstream from Buena Vista.

The Arkansas is the festive whitewater playground of the Rocky Mountain West. There's no better place for a full mix of Class 3–5 rafting and kayaking with all the amenities to match: public access, campgrounds, commercial outfitters, paddling schools for kayakers and stand-up paddleboards, shuttle services, slalom gates, trails, restaurants, urban whitewater play spots for paddlers and tubers, and whole towns dedicated to river recreation.

With frequent road access and an abandoned or active railroad alongside, including relics of old construction in some places, this is no wilderness. Overnight camping possibilities are lean, but if you want to pack up the car and take a whitewater vacation with all the conveniences and support one might imagine, look no further. With all those conveniences come crowded summer weekends—and weeks. The beauty and exhilarating rapids draw 330,000 boaters annually on all reaches, making this the most popular whitewater paddling river in the United States.

Pick your pleasure—Class 2–5 through the 100-mile corridor where the beehive of activity is managed by the Colorado Parks and Wildlife Department, with significant frontage in public ownership under the Bureau of Land Management (BLM). Much of the corridor is essentially a whitewater state park.

Much of the river lies in an unusual canyon, but views of the 14,000-foot Collegiate Peaks of the Sawatch Range and also the southerly Sangre de Cristo Range appear, especially in the Stone Bridge to Vallie Bridge section. Though boaters dominate, this is also a state-designated Gold Medal trout fishery, and some outfitters cater to angling trips by raft or driftboat. Peak flows in June make for intense paddling; lower levels later define the Arkansas as

one of the most technical rock-dodging challenges in the Rockies. River levels drop too low for rafts when upriver irrigation diversions take more water starting August 15.

From top to bottom, boaters gravitate to six different runs and various combinations of them:

➡ The Numbers: These 6 mythic miles of Class 4 rock-studded rapids are reached by gravel roads and a rough access lane south of Granite and north of Buena Vista.

➡ The Fractions, Narrows, and Buena Vista: These sections include 17 miles of Class 2–4 from Railroad Bridge to Buena Vista and beyond.

➡ Browns Canyon: These 11 miles are the choice run for most boaters, Class 3–4 from Ruby Mountain access, south of Buena Vista and Highway 289, with takeout at Hecla Junction in 7 miles or onward through a steep Class 4 drop to Stone Bridge above Salida. Boating here is fun and demanding but not as difficult as The Numbers or Royal Gorge. This is the wildest reach, with sculptural rock formations and no roads alongside. A national monument rising on river left was designated for protection in 2015 after an effective campaign of public support led by outfitter Bill Dvorak, who has been guiding commercial trips here since 1984.

OPPOSITE: With some of the most technical and continuous rapids that are regularly run in the West, the Arkansas foams down through The Numbers and then continues with lively whitewater through The Fractions, The Narrows, the river parkway of Buena Vista, and beyond.

The Arkansas's most popular whitewater is in Browns Canyon. Here a monsoon season rainstorm in August darkens the sky and makes this legendary sequence of rapids look all the wilder.

- Stone Bridge (above Salida) to Vallie Bridge (5 miles above Cotopaxi): These 28 miles offer Class 2–4 with multiple accesses along Highway 50. The first 9 miles, Stone Bridge to Salida, are one of few summerlong, Class 2+ canoe trips through Rocky Mountain highcountry, though portage of a steep raft-chute passage around a low dam above Salida is recommended.

- Parkdale Canyon: These 27 miles are Class 3–4 from Vallie Bridge to Parkdale along Highway 50. The full 55 miles from Stone Bridge to Parkdale offer a three-day whitewater trip with hundreds of lively rapids, though campsites are few and the road crowds the south shore.

- Royal Gorge: Nine miles of Class 4–5 conclude the Arkansas's rapids. This intense extended flume of whitewater disappears into a slot of darkened topography—one of the West's most extreme canyons. Vertical cliffs veering up 1,100 feet cramp this sizable river into jets of runoff only twenty-five feet wide in places. Rapids crowded on one side by an active railroad end where the Arkansas abruptly exits the Rocky Mountains above Cañon City, leaving hundreds of miles below to dewatering, dams, and other transformations the whole way to the Mississippi.

A relatively calm interlude of Class 2-3 Arkansas rapids below Highway 285 leads to the Browns Canyon put-in at Ruby Mountain Campground.

FOLLOWING SPREAD: The Arkansas River dramatically exits Colorado's Rocky Mountains through Royal Gorge—one of the deepest sheer-wall canyons of the West.

SNAKE RIVER | Wyoming

LENGTH: 6 to 78 miles

WHITEWATER: Class 2-4

SEASON: summer to fall

GAUGE: Moose (upper river), Alpine (lower canyon)

PERMIT: yes, in Grand Teton National Park but not limited in number; also for groups of fifteen people or more downstream in Bridger-Teton National Forest

CAMPING: yes, but restricted

OUTFITTERS: guided trips, rental rafts

HIGHLIGHTS: mountain scenery, wildlife, whitewater in Alpine Canyon

Upstream from Jackson, the Snake River sweeps through Grand Teton National Park and frames some of the most spectacular river and mountain views in America.

The Snake River is America's foremost example of a full-bodied river flowing through spectacular scenery of the Rocky Mountains, and no other trip offers this chance to see charismatic megafauna. Meanwhile, the lower section of this reach offers some of the West's most popular whitewater—a rare runnable river with big flows at high elevations in the mountains. Though seldom done as such, and with limited camping opportunities, the entire free-flowing extravaganza can be boated continuously, encompassing some of the best that the Rockies have to offer.

Downstream from Jackson Lake Dam, the Snake can only be described as the ultimate scenic river. The abrupt escarpment of the Teton Range rises point-blank to the west, and for much of the 52-mile float to South Park Bridge (downstream of Jackson), the river delights and overwhelms anyone who appreciates the Tetons' skyscraping climax of the Rockies.

Thanks to an outsized Pleistocene flowage that disgorged from glaciers in the Yellowstone region, the upper Snake's path is broad, braided, and swift but without abrupt rapids. The bifurcating channel through cottonwood, willow, and spruce forests is likewise one of the West's wildlife hot spots. Moose, bison, beavers, and bald eagles are often seen from the water or from shoreline excursions, while elk, bears, and coyotes occasionally appear. Some outfitters offer wildlife floats at daybreak.

Riffling through Grand Teton National Park for 27 miles below the dam, several sections are floated by 70,000 rafters, canoeists, and kayakers per year. The Park Service requires permits, available without reservations for a fee at the Moose Visitor Center, with no limit on numbers. Riverfront camping in the park is not allowed.

The first section, 5 miles of Class 1 whitewater from Jackson Lake Dam to Pacific Creek, is the easiest, with great views and nominal hazards.

Next, 10 miles from Pacific Creek to Deadman's Bar is Class 1–2 and considered "intermediate" because of swift flow and tree snags.

For 10 more miles from Deadman's Bar to Moose, Class 2 boating is considered "advanced" by the park because fast current, brush, and logjams can be troublesome to the unwary and even the cautious. Dynamic channels open new passages and abandon others as traps of upended trees. To anticipate hazards and plan a few strategic moves, check with park rangers when getting your permit.

From the lower section of the national park at the Moose ramp, it's 14 miles of swift water with log hazards possible to the Wilson Bridge west of Jackson, followed by 14 miles to South Park Bridge with fast flow and gravel islands.

First built for ranchland and then for homes, levees below the park constrain flows, reduce riparian floodplains, restrict groundwater, eliminate wetlands, and reshape the morphology of the riverbed into a flumelike rush that erodes islands and banks. Even so, the river remains a scenic float for rafts, canoes, and driftboats, and is popular among anglers. Camping is limited but possible at some BLM islands and shores.

From the South Park Bridge to West Table Creek, the Snake continues with Class 2 rapids in a 19-mile transition zone—prelude to the constricted canyon ahead. Bridger-Teton National Forest camping is allowed only in developed roadside campgrounds, May through Labor Day.

Finally, the 8-mile plunge through Alpine Canyon is an American classic and one of the West's most popular whitewater destinations, with 165,000 floaters per year. From West Table Creek access to Sheep Gulch ramp, the Snake funnels into riotous drops with waves and holes, including the famed Lunch Counter and Big Kahuna Rapids. This is principally a raft and kayak river, but it is also suited to expert canoeists on lower flows beginning in late July or so. Highway 26 parallels with steady traffic but lies mostly out of sight. Use is heavy; for a quieter adventure, avoid summertime Fridays and Saturdays.

Taken together, these reaches of the Snake offer one of the best road-accessible river vacations anywhere.

The Snake River enters Alpine
Canyon with powerful whitewater.
Among the most-floated rivers
in the West, it is also one of few
major streams offering summerlong
boating at high elevations.

SNAKE RIVER | Idaho · Oregon

ROCKY MOUNTAINS

LENGTH: 79 miles, Hells Canyon Dam to Heller Bar; shorter and longer trips possible

WHITEWATER: Class 3-4, big volume

SEASON: spring, summer, fall

GAUGE: Hells Canyon Dam

PERMIT: yes, and limited from late May to mid-September

CAMPING: yes

OUTFITTERS: guided trips

HIGHLIGHTS: big-volume whitewater, deep canyon, fishing, spring and fall trips

Far downstream from the Snake River's Wyoming headwaters, Hells Canyon is one of the deepest canyons in America and has the highest-volume whitewater in the West next to the Grand Canyon of the Colorado. On 17,000 cfs, Bill Sedivy, former director of Idaho Rivers United, leads the way through breaking waves.

While Grand Teton National Park and Jackson Hole, Wyoming, draw boaters to the Snake River's headwaters, Hells Canyon awaits 800 miles downstream. Here the Snake powers through America's second-deepest canyon with whitewater that's second only to the Grand Canyon in volume of flow. The pent-up river is released from Hells Canyon Dam with summer flows of 12,000 cfs or more. Difficulty increases at 20,000 cfs, and springtime floods up to 60,000 cfs create an otherworldly sense of hydraulic scale.

The river below the dam swirls with suspiciously quiet but ominously hidden force. Then in 6 miles at Wild Sheep Rapid, all fury breaks loose as the accumulated runoff from hundreds of miles upstream consolidates into one explosive rapid. Following a smooth-water tongue as green as mint jelly, the flow collides with white foam against black basalt boulders forcing boaters to pull hard to the right. In 2 more miles, Granite Rapid follows with a similar rollicking route, and other sizable rapids come later.

The canyon's cleavage splits the Wallowa Mountains of Oregon from the Seven Devils Mountains of Idaho. Hells Canyon is often cited as the deepest in America, though the Sierra Nevada tower 8,000 feet over both sides of the Middle Fork Kings in California while the Snake's canyon at one point rises 5,620 feet on the Oregon side and 7,900 feet on the Idaho side. But Hells Canyon is longer than the Kings, and its steep walls overwhelm with an essence of enormity: voluminous flow, depth from rim to floor, height of cliffs, and size of boulders.

Layers of Columbian basalt and metamorphic rocks rise up in cake layers of contrasting colors. Lower steps of this grand topography stand starkly bare in harsh aridity, while the terraces above sport

sculpted ponderosa pines among golden grasses, then clusters of evergreens, and finally scented forests of Douglas firs that ramp on to Rocky Mountain–like heights hidden from river view by intervening ridges and subsummits.

Vast beaches of the predam era have been reduced radically since upstream reservoirs trapped sand and silt that had earlier settled instead on bars downstream. But some minor beaches remain, especially below the mouth of the Salmon River, which still peaks in uncontrolled floods. Lingering groves of hackberry or alders here and there offer welcome shade from the summer sun's blaze that inspired this canyon's name.

Like other features, the canyon's temperatures register extreme. Spring arrives gloriously when the arid slopes tint green with sprouting grasses. Summer sizzles with little shade but delightful conditions on the water. Fall arrives sharply luxurious with cooler days but lingering warmth into October. Fishing is good for bass. Chinook salmon, listed as threatened under the Endangered Species Act, still spawn in the main stem below Hells Canyon Dam, and white sturgeon—North America's largest freshwater fish—survive in numbers oppressively limited by dams upstream and down.

The Forest Service requires and rations permits by lottery during summer. Spring and fall permits, self-issued, are not limited. Autumn boating here is a great option.

At Pittsburg Landing, 31 miles below the put-in, a gravel road wends its way down to a ramp and campground where some boaters take out. However, 48 more miles entice boaters on to Heller Bar, south of Clarkston. For the full experience—though few do it—float onward from Heller Bar for 26 miles with longer pools and easier rapids that run nearly to Hells Gate State Park ramp in Lewiston before terminally stalling in the backwater of Lower Granite Dam.

Hells Canyon is also the choice destination of jet boaters who motor there in strong numbers.

Tour boats packed with dozens of passengers breeze up and down, and private boats roar by on weekends. Fewer venture into the formidable rapids above Pittsburg Landing, so many oar-powered boaters prefer that upper section.

After decades of inequity when nonmotorized craft were limited by permit restrictions but jet boats increased without regulation, new rules in the 1990s imposed some limits on powerboats, including specified days when they're banned above Pittsburg Landing. Call Hells Canyon National Recreation Area for seasonal details.

Before 1967 the free-flowing Snake through Hells Canyon totaled twice its current length. Dams built by Idaho Power Company then inundated the upper half. Then the ultimate megadam was slated for construction, first below the Salmon River confluence and then above it. River supporters in Oregon and Idaho organized to defeat the proposal in the nick of time, and Congress designated the remaining length of Hells Canyon a National Wild and Scenic River in 1975. The remaining river is daily pulsed by high and low releases from the hydroelectric dams upstream; boaters must beware of suddenly fluctuating levels.

Many river runners are drawn less to Hells Canyon than other great western trips owing to the jet boat intrusion, summer heat, and tidal releases from the dams upstream, but no other river outside the Southwest matches the Snake's combination of grandeur, volume, and arid beauty, and it occupies a class by itself in the geography of American waterways.

The Snake River in Hells Canyon churns over shoreline rocks at the mouth of Saddle Creek, downstream from Granite Rapid.

SALMON RIVER | Idaho

LENGTH: 78 miles for River of No Return section; other trips up to 420 miles

WHITEWATER: Class 2-4

SEASON: summer, fall

GAUGE: Shoup; White Bird for lower river

PERMIT: yes, for the River of No Return section, June 20 to September 7

CAMPING: yes

OUTFITTERS: guided trips

HIGHLIGHTS: wilderness, rapids, salmon, campsites, best ultralong trip

Typical of larger drops on the Salmon, Vinegar Creek Rapid plunges with breaking waves and pour-over boulders.

FOLLOWING SPREAD: Rapids of the lower Salmon offer wave trains on sizable flows all summer and fall while delectable sandbars line the shores. Wapshilla Rapid foams 8 miles above the Salmon's confluence with the Snake River.

The Salmon River's multiday wilderness trip offers stirring whitewater, irresistible campsites, wildlife, hot springs, hiking trails, delectable summer weather, and strong flows continuing through autumn. In short, this stream has all that one might desire in a wild river vacation or pilgrimage.

This may be the perfect weeklong expedition. It's hard to imagine a better river for rowing through splendid days and then pulling up to a sandy beach and camping in the shade of aged ponderosa pines with a view to green water and a mountain-canyon paradise. June is cool with high flows; July and August are hot; autumn is invigorating on lower flows with balmy weather until October.

The usual trip is through a section called the "River of No Return," as penned by Lewis and Clark, who were turned back by whitewater—likely Pine Creek Rapid below the North Fork—and forced overland. This classic section runs 78 miles from Corn Creek to Vinegar Creek. Whitewater pushes hard but mostly in straightforward routes. A nonintuitive move comes midway at Big Mallard Rapid; scout and stay extreme left. Wildfires have charred much of this route in past decades, leaving forests in a burned and unburned mosaic while green growth recovers.

Permits are required, in high demand, and rationed by lottery from the Forest Service. Quotas are not limited before June 20 or after September 7.

The lower Salmon also makes for an excellent trip of 132 miles from Vinegar Creek to Heller Bar ramp, with the final 20 miles through Hells Canyon of the Snake. Shorter trips on the lower Salmon are popular from Riggins (102 miles) or Hammer Creek (70 miles) to Heller Bar. This is dry country, with rugged walls rising to Rocky Mountain

heights, sandy campsites, powerful summerlong flows, and a signature attraction of absolutely fabulous wave trains. In spring, at flows above 20,000 cfs, Slide Rapid—4 miles above the Snake River—unconditionally flips all rafts and cannot be portaged; avoid lower Salmon trips at that or higher water levels! At normal summer flows this peculiar rapid does not exist at all.

Permits for the lower Salmon are not reserved ahead of time or limited in number, so for boaters who are inclined to schedule on impulse—or fail to score the permit they wanted—this makes a default adventure comparable in quality to some of the other great rivers of the West.

Enticing but seldom run as a contiguous trip, a 170-mile reach from the upper Salmon, starting below the breached Sunbeam Dam near Stanley and ending at Corn Creek, offers a medley of mostly Class 2 and some Class 3 whitewater with captivating views, cottonwood forests, and roads that share the valley and canyon corridors but intrude little on the overall atmosphere. In fact, the lack of other boating traffic might make up for ranches and cars here and there.

For adventurers looking for the finest super-extended trip in America, a total of 420 miles can be run from below Sunbeam Dam's remains to Lewiston on the Snake River. This requires a well-timed permit for the River of No Return reach or, easier, an orchestrated arrival at Corn Creek in September after the permit season closes. Resupply is easy with a walk at the riverfront towns of Salmon and Riggins. This ultimate river trip tours eight major subranges of the Rockies, transects the largest wilderness in forty-eight states, and lacks the flatwater and buggy intervals encountered on the comparably long Green River.

The entire Salmon, from Sawtooth Valley headwaters to the Snake, is also America's longest river outside Alaska with no dams, though at the

headwaters a weir for the Sawtooth Fish Hatchery requires a short portage.

Once nourishing the greatest spawning runs of Chinook salmon on earth, the Salmon River's anadromous fish now confront massive dams on the lower Columbia and then four 100-foot-tall dams on the Snake River below the Salmon's mouth. Serving little defensible purpose, those four dams require enormous subsidies and are driving salmon toward extinction, which all makes a strong economic, biological, and ethical case for dam removal—the goal of the Save Our Wild Salmon Coalition, Idaho Rivers United, and other groups.

OPPOSITE: River running on the Salmon can begin below the Sawtooth Mountains town of Stanley and continue past eight subranges of the Rockies while penetrating the largest wilderness areas in the lower forty-eight states. Here in the heart of wild Idaho, a trail from the Warren Creek campsite leads to a view downstream.

The Salmon River reflects twilight at a serene campsite downstream from Salmon.

SALMON RIVER, MIDDLE FORK | Idaho

LENGTH: 100 miles, including 4 miles on the main-stem Salmon

WHITEWATER: Class 3-4

SEASON: summer, low-water trips in fall

GAUGE: Middle Fork Lodge

PERMIT: yes, and in high demand

CAMPING: yes

OUTFITTERS: guided trips

HIGHLIGHTS: long wilderness trip, whitewater, spectacular campsites, hot springs

The Middle Fork of the Salmon is the favorite multiday river trip of many experienced boaters. From the deeply forested start in the heart of Idaho's Rocky Mountains, this fluid jewel tumbles northward in a delightful stairstep of Class 3 and 4 rapids challenging rafters, kayakers, and expert canoeists typically depending on raft support for their gear. High flows of early summer create long continuous rapids. By July moderating levels offer exquisite whitewater.

Campsites, hot springs, wildlife, and hiking trails up tributary canyons are all big draws here. Chinook salmon still return to the Middle Fork and its pristine tributaries to spawn. Most of the mileage passes through the River of No Return Wilderness, which adjoins similar preserves of central Idaho for the greatest concentration of wilderness areas outside Alaska.

Every day brings a new series of intricate whitewater passages and striking views through the length of rock-walled canyons interspersed with pine-shaded benches and ridgelines of mountains ramping up toward high peaks.

Permits in summertime are coveted and obtained by Forest Service lottery. The chances of success are slim; many boaters apply year after year hoping for the trip of their dreams, or they organize in parties with everyone applying for a permit. Signing on with an outfitter is the other option for those who can pay and are content to not paddle or row their own craft. Going in August, and either rock picking for 25 miles to Indian Creek or flying in to that backcountry airstrip are other options to increase the chance for a permit.

The usual put-in, north of Stanley and just below Dagger Falls, drops boaters directly into upper river excitement. With takeout on the main-stem Salmon River at Cache Bar, 4 miles below the Middle Fork confluence, the full 100-mile run typically takes a week.

Wildlife biologists John and Frank Craighead rafted here in the 1950s and popularized the term "wild river." They later expanded the concept as they first crafted the fundamentals of the National Wild and Scenic Rivers System, which included the Middle Fork as one of its original members in 1968.

Topping many river runners' wish lists, the Middle Fork Salmon has an unequaled mix of exciting rapids, wilderness, seductive campsites, hot springs, wildlife, and unmarred Rocky Mountain beauty. This riffle leads to a campsite at Sheep Creek.

FOLLOWING SPREAD: Tappan Falls on the Middle Fork Salmon is a good ride on the low levels of late summer.

SELWAY RIVER | Idaho

LENGTH: 47 miles

WHITEWATER: Class 4

SEASON: June to early July; high water can be hazardous until late June

GAUGE: Lowell

PERMIT: yes, for early summer, and very hard to get

CAMPING: yes

OUTFITTERS: guided trips

HIGHLIGHTS: one of the wildest rivers, difficult rapids, fishing, pristine water

The Selway is the wildest of four renowned Idaho river trips and traverses the deeply forested Selway-Bitterroot Wilderness. It also has the most challenging rapids and crystalline water quality.

Among seasoned western river runners, a special awe surfaces at the simple mention of the Selway. Some value this trip even more than the Grand Canyon and the Middle Fork Salmon. Arriving at the put-in campground called Paradise, anticipation is palpable among boaters rigging their craft for the five-day excursion.

Snow keeps the access road closed through May. Early June presents high flows with some of the most continuously difficult whitewater regularly run in the West. Facing hazardous consequences of a flip and a long swim in meltwater, early season boating is only for experts in strong teams.

The narrow window of late June through early July offers lower levels for advanced boaters. As the water recedes, intricate rapids demand complex routing around boulders. The most challenging drops come after Moose Creek, 27 miles below Paradise. By mid-July the level often recedes too low for normal rafting—traditionally 1,200 cfs at the lower end of the run.

Salmon and steelhead that surmount the eight dams downstream on the Columbia and Snake Rivers still make their way back to rich spawning grounds of the Selway and its pristine tributaries. Fishing, hiking, and campsites are premier, and the Selway has the added appeal of great snorkeling in transparent (but cold!) water.

Recognizing that a range of river experiences are needed, and that the Selway is a small stream easily marred by overuse, the Forest Service rations recreation to maintain the aura of true wilderness with one trip daily—America's only river so effectively regulated for solitude. Consequently the chances of getting the required lottery permit are fewer than one in forty; along with the Grand Canyon, this is the hardest permit to score.

Permits are not required after the water drops in August, so low-flow trips, congested with boulders, are an option for skilled paddlers in kayaks, I-Ks, or perhaps small rafts. Others who want to see this forested green passage can hike the Selway River Trail for 50 miles from Paradise to the takeout.

The float trip ends at Race Creek, a mile above unrunnable Selway Falls. Downstream from there a scenic day trip can be enjoyed to the Middle Fork Clearwater, below the Selway's confluence with the Lochsa, which follows a similar Class 4–5 course, though its corridor is shared with Highway 12.

With challenges of difficult whitewater, remoteness, permit scarcity, and a long shuttle, the Selway is a rare experience for avid boaters.

In early summer the Selway River offers one of the West's outstanding five-day trips with challenging whitewater through wilderness.

FOLLOWING SPREAD: The Selway rushes through rapids below Moose Creek.

FLATHEAD RIVER, NORTH FORK | Montana

LENGTH: 11 to 58 miles

WHITEWATER: Class 2, one section Class 2+ or 3

SEASON: summer; extended through fall on the lower North Fork

GAUGE: British Columbia border (upper), Columbia Falls (lower)

PERMIT: no, but camping permits for east-bank sites in Glacier National Park

CAMPING: yes

OUTFITTERS: guided trips

HIGHLIGHTS: clear water, colorful riverbed, mountain scenery, wildlife

Sunshine burns morning mist off the North Fork Flathead at a cobble-bar campsite near Red Meadow Creek. The Livingston Range of Glacier National Park rises in the background.

The North Fork Flathead, from Canada to the Middle Fork confluence north of Columbia Falls, is one of America's finest extended canoe trips and one of a select group with scenery of high Rocky Mountain peaks shining in the distance. Experienced paddlers need not be whitewater experts, and this is also an easy raft trip.

Crystal clear runoff varnishes metamorphic rocks in mosaics of black, white, red, and blue. Along with the Flathead's South and Middle Forks, this is the most brilliantly colorful riverbed anywhere. Rounding out the chromatic rainbow, pools reflect the deepest blue green. Spacious gravel bars with highcountry views make seductive campsites. Rapids are uncommonly easy for a river in such a mountainous region. Extensive forest fires have raged through the valley in recent years; starkly beautiful remains are evident especially along the lower river.

The entire course below British Columbia headwaters marks the boundary between Glacier National Park to the east and Flathead National Forest. The first 25 miles south of Canada wind sharply to an access at Polebridge. Larger below, with ample flows through the fall, the North Fork continues for 18 miles to Big Creek access, another 11 miles to Glacier Rim access, and then 4 miles to the Middle Fork confluence and a ramp at Blankenship Bridge.

Rapids are mostly swift wave trains and tight bends, while fallen trees pose hazards for the unwary in the upper half of the run. The easiest reach is Polebridge to Big Creek; the most challenging is Big Creek to Glacier Rim access, with four Class 2+ rapids and one Class 3-.

OPPOSITE: A peaceful evening descends on the North Fork Flathead upstream from Camas Creek. Sourced in Canada, this river provides one of the West's finest multiday canoe voyages or an easy raft trip through mountain country.

Sunrise warms a North Fork Flathead camp above Camas Creek. The starkly beautiful remains of burned trees spike the mountainsides while new growth takes hold.

Springtime in the northern Rockies arrives late, and ice-cold runoff lingering through early summer delays the season for enthralling swimming in this crystal clear water (take a mask and snorkel!), so most boaters wait until July or so to launch. The weather often holds into autumn, with adequate flows below Polebridge while cottonwoods turn gold. The gravel access road north of Columbia Falls promises miles of dusty washboard, but it is seldom noticed from the water.

Anglers cast for native cutthroat trout, though owing to the river's glacial sources, low nutrients mean small fish. Rare native bull trout grow larger but must be released. Wildlife sightings may include moose, otter, deer, and bald eagles. Wolves might be seen or heard at night. Precautions should be taken for grizzly bears, including food canisters and spotless camping protocols, especially on the national park's east bank.

The Flathead's other two forks are also exceptional but more difficult. Pure wilderness, the Middle Fork's upper 32 miles require flying or packing in, while the lower 41 miles offer athletic Class 2–4 road-accessible whitewater. The South Fork's elegant wilderness run starts with a pack trip to upper reaches. Rafters confront an unrunnable narrow gorge at the lower end of this trip, which requires a significant portage or pack trip out. Below that, and accessible by gravel road, a 15-mile Class 2 canoe run is launched after a quarter-mile carry to the Cedar Flats put-in and ends above Hungry Horse Reservoir.

A family of rafters drifts on North Fork Flathead rapids below Big Creek.

SOUTHWEST

While the water in rivers always comes from somewhere else—upstream—this reality is stark and vivid with desert rivers. Most of their flow begins in distant mountains, and the sensational contrast of frothing water in arid canyons stirs curiosity and delight. The desert rivers at first sight just don't seem possible! But they make for spectacular boating among towering walls of stone, through turbulent rapids where tributary streams have deposited bed loads of rock during flood flows, and where a radiant quality of light warms red-rock slopes and waters nourish a green edge of cottonwoods, willows, and even saguaro cacti above Arizona's southernmost streams.

Canyons are the big draw, and so the greatest draw is the Grand Canyon of the Colorado. Nothing competes with its sublime walls, length of wildness, and big thundering waters. The river's gravitas rises from prodigious Rocky Mountain snowmelt combined with the Colorado Plateau's bold layers of sandstone thousands of feet thick.

Other desert rivers beckon as well. Desolation Canyon of the Green River is magnificent and more accessible than the Grand Canyon for river runners. The Yampa, White, San Juan, Dolores, Salt, Rio Grande, and Rio Chama all offer fine trips through desert wilds.

With relative scarcity of towns, roads, and access, many desert rivers are done as multiday trips. Some of the best and longest river sojourns are found here: the Green for 377 miles, the Colorado for a midriver reach of 233 miles, and the Grand Canyon for 280 miles.

A few desert rivers in southern Arizona and Texas appeal to boaters all winter, but even there, cold snaps can lacquer ice on the oars. Springtime bursts early with pleasure as the waters rise and weather warms. Summer is frying-pan hot, with river splash the ideal relief. Where flows remain strong, autumn enthralls as the days shorten and the nights chill with downdrafts from highcountry above.

GREEN RIVER | Utah • Colorado

LENGTH: 7 to 377 miles; popular trips run 7, 45, 68, and 84 miles

WHITEWATER: Class 1-4

SEASON: late spring, summer, fall

GAUGE: Jensen, Green River

PERMIT: yes, separately for Lodore-Split Mountain, Desolation-Gray, and Labyrinth-Stillwater Canyons, and limited in number

CAMPING: yes

OUTFITTERS: guided trips for Lodore-Split Mountain, Desolation-Gray, and Labyrinth-Stillwater Canyons

HIGHLIGHTS: deep canyons, hiking, campsites, whitewater

PREVIOUS SPREAD: At sunset, Desolation Canyon of the Green River in Utah glows golden at the Upper Three Canyon campsite.

The Green River boils at Hell's Half Mile Rapid in Lodore Canyon.

FOLLOWING SPREAD: The Green River of Utah and Colorado runs dam-free for 377 boatable miles. Here it cuts through Lodore Canyon with red-rock walls and slopes of juniper, pinyon, and sage.

Epic in every way, the Green River from Flaming Gorge Dam in Utah to the Colorado River confluence offers an extended outing unmatched in the desert regions of the West. It's usually run as a series of excellent shorter trips. Outside Alaska, only the Salmon River is longer for total length of undammed flow. Few rivers offer similar qualities of sublime canyon depths, arid wilderness, desert campsites, side-canyon hikes, pictographs, and moderate rapids.

Runnable water extends for 377 miles from Flaming Gorge Dam to the river's mouth, and prepared boaters can continue on the Colorado River for Cataract Canyon's 15 miles of Class 4 rapids followed by 33 miles of reservoir to Hite Marina.

Below Flaming Gorge Dam, the Green through Red Canyon is popular among day trippers and anglers, and the summertime put-in is often mobbed. No permit is needed, but at busy times boats must be inflated off river and driven to the ramp. Eight miles of clear water with Class 2 rapids and world-renowned trout fishing in chilled tailwaters of the dam lead to the Little Hole takeout. Boaters can continue with gentle riffles for another 38 miles looping through picturesque Browns Park, Colorado, to the entrance of Lodore Canyon in Dinosaur National Monument.

In the famed Lodore, 19 miles of red-rock cliffs tier up 2,000 feet while Class 2 rapids and three forceful Class 3–4 drops cleave the Uinta Mountains—the largest east-west-oriented range in America. Permits and reserved campsites are required from the National Park Service.

Lodore's terminus at Echo Park marks the site of one of the most notable American dam fights. A proposal to flood both the Green and Yampa Rivers here in Dinosaur National Monument was

defeated in 1956, establishing a new precedent of not allowing dams in units of the national park system (the dam proposal was moved downstream to Glen Canyon on the Colorado and built). Looming over Echo Park, Steamboat Rock rises 800 feet—one of the most dramatic landforms towering over any river in America.

This Green River trip continues downstream for another 17 miles of swift rapids in Whirlpool Canyon and then 9 more miles of steeper, big-volume Class 2–3 in Split Mountain Canyon, where the antecedent river predated the mountains' uplift, giving today's boaters a tour of the excavated center of a mountain with craggy outcrops and dramatic ridgelines. The Lodore-Whirlpool-Split Mountain trip of 45 miles ends at the Dinosaur National Monument ramp north of Jensen, Utah.

Next, a seldom-boated, 100-mile reach of the Green flows from Split Mountain to the entrance of Desolation Canyon. All Class 1, this reach passes the mouth of the White River and almost encircles stately sandstone buttes at Horseshoe Bend. In springtime the river overflows its banks and then recedes slowly from floodplains that breed mosquitoes like no other place in the American desert; while the scenery is captivating, mosquitoes and flies can be oppressive through summer months. Boaters may need to wear a headnet while rowing this section and minimize time ashore. Autumn would be a better time for this quiet journey.

Dirt-road access to Sand Wash marks the put-in for Desolation Canyon. Melding continuously with Gray Canyon, this 84-mile reach is one of the desert region's gems, and Bureau of Land Management (BLM) permits are limited.

"Deso" might be considered an easier iteration of the Grand Canyon: the inner gorge is spectacular but not as awesome, the rapids are lively but not as steep, the permit is in demand but not as difficult to get, and the length of the trip is significant but not as great. Minor rapids and twelve Class 2+ and 3+ drops spice a route with tempting campsites, hiking

The Green River cuts its dramatic path through the center of Split Mountain.

OPPOSITE: In Dinosaur National Monument, a high rocky perch offers a view to the Green River carving its passage through Split Mountain.

opportunities up many of the sixty side canyons, and a feeling of resounding wildness through the West's largest wilderness study area, threatened by additional oil and gas leasing on public land.

Below the usual Desolation-Gray Canyon takeout at Swasey's Beach, the river pitches over a runnable diversion weir and flows 9 more miles to Interstate 70 at Green River, where grocery re-supply is possible, and onward with gentle flows suitable for canoes through another 120 miles to the Colorado River. BLM permits are required here for Labyrinth Canyon.

A cliffhanger dirt road switchbacks to river level on the east side at Mineral Bottom, 68 miles downstream from Green River at the end of Labyrinth, where most paddlers take out. No other road access occurs between the town of Green River and Hite Marina, downstream in the reservoir formed by Glen Canyon Dam on the Colorado River. For those continuing beyond Mineral Bottom and through Stillwater Canyon to the end of the Green River, Canyonlands National Park requires a camping permit.

Though pricey—and significantly more expensive for rafts than canoes—floaters can arrange for a motorboat shuttle from the Green and Colorado Rivers confluence back up the languid Colorado to Moab, thus avoiding 15 miles of whitewater downstream in the Colorado's Cataract Canyon (permit required) and 33 miles of reservoir to Hite (see Colorado River).

Created perhaps 1,000 years ago, impressive petroglyphs by American Indians of the Fremont culture can still be seen above the Green River near the Desolation Canyon tributary of Flat Canyon (top left). Thunderstorms brew in the background of the Green River at Upheaval Bottom in Labyrinth Canyon (bottom left).

OPPOSITE: Steamboat Rock rises monumentally at the confluence of the Yampa and Green Rivers.

YAMPA RIVER | Colorado

LENGTH: 71 miles, including 27 miles on the Green River

WHITEWATER: Class 3-4

SEASON: late spring, early summer, low-water trips later

GAUGE: Deerlodge Park

PERMIT: yes, and limited

CAMPING: yes

OUTFITTERS: guided trips

HIGHLIGHTS: sandstone canyon, great campsites

If you're looking for a classic sheer-wall canyon of the West, with smooth sandstone jutting up to blue sky while the river lures you around enchanted bends, the lower Yampa is near the top of the list.

Boaters kick off from Deerlodge ramp in northwestern Colorado and follow the river's incised path while walls of Weber Sandstone rise higher and higher. At Tiger Wall, desert varnish of black, orange, and white oxidation stripes the cliff faces. Rapids enliven this run with flushes of early summer runoff. The big drop, Warm Springs, was formed overnight by a landslide in 1965.

Rafters embark May through June and later on years of heavy snowpack. By mid-July flows typically recede too low for rafts but stay suitable for kayaks. Lacking its push in midsummer, this is a good canyon cruise for experienced canoeists. National Park Service permits, with substantial fees, are in heavy demand until July.

Campsites on sandbars and cottonwood-shaded benches await. Harding Hole delights with overhanging cliffs soaring 1,000 feet, reached by a south-bank trail. The Yampa empties into the Green River at Echo Park where Steamboat Rock juts monumentally skyward.

From there the trip continues on the Green River for 17 miles through Whirlpool Canyon to Rainbow Park ramp and then 9 more miles through Split Mountain Canyon to Dinosaur National Monument's ramp upstream from Jensen, Utah.

After escaping the specter of Echo Park Dam in the 1950s, the next threat to the Yampa came with the Juniper-Cross Mountain proposal for dual hydropower dams upstream of Deerlodge. These were halted in the 1980s, though the Yampa lacks permanent protection in the National Wild and Scenic Rivers System.

Rafts ply serene waters of the Yampa River below Harding Hole—a quintessential red-rock canyon of the West.

COLORADO RIVER | Colorado · Utah

LENGTH: 6 to 120 miles, plus 112 miles of river (and reservoir) possible below

WHITEWATER: Class 1–2, plus Class 4 in Westwater and Cataract Canyons

SEASON: spring, summer, fall

GAUGE: Utah state line

PERMIT: yes, for Westwater and Cataract Canyons; camping permit for Ruby-Horsethief Canyon

CAMPING: yes

OUTFITTERS: guided trips, rental craft for some sections

HIGHLIGHTS: extended trip, whitewater, gentle flows, wild canyons, easy access

The infamous Skull Rapid in Westwater Canyon of the Colorado requires an urgent move from right to left to miss the hydraulic hole capable of flipping rafts in the center of the river.

FOLLOWING SPREAD: After descending the west slope of the Rocky Mountains, the Colorado River pushes its silty volume past an ancient outcrop called Black Rocks in Ruby-Horsethief Canyon, downstream from Loma.

The very name, Colorado River, evokes a sense of myth, powerful whitewater, and a sweep of dramatic landforms from glaciated summits at the Continental Divide to the grandest of desert canyons. Epic, intriguing, forbidding—all describe the path this artery takes as one of ten major rivers radiating from the highcountry soul of the West, and none compares to this river in its journey from Rocky Mountain peaks to Great Basin Desert, from cliffhanger trails to interstate highways, and from hardscrabble towns of oil boom-and-bust to trendy destinations for leisure. This river storms through four states and 1,450 miles, ending in Mexico's Gulf of California. Upper reaches, not covered in this book, drop from highcountry to cross northcentral Colorado and include intense rapids, several moderate reaches, and a number of dams and diversions.

Below those, 120 miles from Palisade (above Grand Junction) to Moab await with a medley of gentle water and tumultuous rapids, altogether a spicy extended trip for rafters or selected runs for kayakers and canoeists. Additional miles, with distinctive problems, await below as well. While the Grand Canyon, much farther downstream, unmistakably ranks as the most renowned big-water wilderness trip in America, this middle reach of the Colorado has variety and invites exploration with the essence of a stream that has been extolled ever since Spanish conquistadors named it for its silty redness.

Various choices await: gentle canyon cruises, blasts of boiling hydraulics, kaleidoscopes of red-rock walls, or a weeklong sojourn combining all of that across the Great American Desert. This middle expanse of the Colorado can be parceled as follows:

→ Palisade to Loma: Launch east (upstream) of Grand Junction at Riverbend Park in Palisade (dams block the river above there) for this Class 1–2 section. For 30 miles the Colorado meanders among cottonwood bars, islands, and the edge of Grand Junction while cliffs of Colorado National Monument dominate to the south.

→ Ruby-Horsethief Canyon (this is local parlance, though Horsethief Canyon comes first, and the two are indistinguishable to most people): High-volume Class 1–2 extends from Loma to Westwater Canyon. Ancient black Precambrian schist underlies tall red sandstone walls in this reach of 27 miles—two easy days to the brink of Westwater Canyon in Utah. Rigorous hiking up Rattlesnake Canyon leads to spectacular wilderness arches like those in Arches National Park. This reach is great for canoes. But no farther!

→ Westwater Canyon: This stretch is Class 4. Get a permit from the BLM in Moab, two months in advance. This 17-mile wilderness rafting run to the takeout near Cisco confronts frothing challenges at a dozen rapids, including Funnel Falls and the notorious Skull Rapid and its Room of Doom eddy—especially threatening above 6,000 cfs in early summer (peaking at 20,000 cfs and dropping to 3,000 cfs in autumn). Scout here on the left, and avoid a frightening hole and entrapping eddy by pulling vigorously right to left.

→ Cisco to Dewey Bridge and Highway 128: Pleasant riffles pass verdant riparian islands among surrounding bluffs and ranchland

for 15 miles in this Class 1–2 section. Though much is private and a bit buggy, this unsung but pretty reach lacks not only development and roads but also other floaters, and thereby offers unexpected solitude.

→ Dewey Bridge to Moab: Big-water Class 2 tours awe-inspiring scenery that overwhelms for 32 miles with some powerful riffles but mostly gentle flows to the Highway 191 bridge near Moab. Though shorter than Westwater on excitement and wilderness, the stunning, Monument Valley–type scenery compensates, offering the desert region's best easily run and readily accessed day trips. Intermediate takeouts make shuttles easy by bike, and campsites also beckon. Views include a parade of monolithic sandstone walls and sheer-sided buttes like visions of an idealized Southwest while the lofty La Sal Mountains rise beyond.

An additional stretch, from Moab to the Green River confluence, is Class 1 for 64 miles but requires a motorboat shuttle back upstream by arrangement with local outfitters—far more expensive for rafts than for canoes or kayaks. Or, below the confluence, skilled and capably outfitted boaters can continue another 15 miles with heavily pounding Class 4 rapids through Cataract Canyon (permit required). But this commits you to a subsequent 33 miles to Hite Marina in the dead water behind Glen Canyon Dam. Some boaters hire tows. I've addressed the dreaded flatwater memorably by rowing in starlight to avoid the quotidian afternoon wall of wind and by sleeping on the boat to evade the reservoir's perimeter of depthless mud.

On tributaries of the middle Colorado, good trips include the Gunnison, which enters the Colorado at Grand Junction. A 16-mile gorge of technical whitewater downstream from Black Canyon of the Gunnison National Park requires four-wheel drive (shuttles available) and a steep

mile-long hike to the put-in, with mules on hire to pack rafts. And, below Westwater, the Dolores River offers a renowned Class 3–4 run through pine-clad canyons and then Class 3 through red rock for 50 miles from Slickrock to Bedrock, though runnable flows rarely occur since McPhee Dam shackled the river upstream in 1984.

Few boaters run the Colorado's full Palisade to Moab reach, but the united trip offers a low-key Colorado River alternative to the Grand Canyon and ranks as one of the longest desert trips with spectacular scenery, wilderness whitewater, and gentle flows with easy access. As an expedition or as a series of weekend adventures, this section of the Colorado showcases a varied desert landscape like few other rivers do.

Sandstone walls of Westwater Canyon warm to early morning sunlight below the Colorado's confluence with the Little Dolores River.

FOLLOWING SPREAD: A kayaker strokes through evening light on the Colorado River as it flows toward the Fisher Towers between Dewey Bridge and Moab (left). The Colorado rushes past sandstone monoliths shaped through eons of erosion by the river and its tributaries above Moab (top right). Tributary to the middle Colorado, the Gunnison River flows from a splendid whitewater gorge where the put-in requires a steep mile-long hike downstream from Black Canyon of the Gunnison National Park (bottom right).

COLORADO RIVER | Arizona

LENGTH: 226 miles, Lee's Ferry to Diamond Creek; 280 miles, Lee's Ferry to Pearce Ferry

WHITEWATER: Class 4–5

SEASON: spring, summer, and fall; cold trips in winter

GAUGE: Lee's Ferry

PERMIT: yes, and difficult to get

CAMPING: yes

OUTFITTERS: guided trips, rental rafts, and complete trip setups with gear and food

HIGHLIGHTS: the grandest canyon, big whitewater, side canyon hikes

Sheer walls of the Grand Canyon rise above Nankoweap Creek, 50 miles below the Lee's Ferry put-in.

The grandest of all canyons has been sculpted by the Colorado River between Lee's Ferry and Lake Mead—the ultimate big-river adventure with the most turbulent rapids that many boaters are ever likely to encounter.

Walls of sandstone, granite, and limestone rise up thousands of feet. Serene and sublime miles are mixed with pulsing flows that rage in waves ten feet tall and with depthless churning holes. Wildness resonates with the overwhelming feeling of a place entirely apart and with primal excitement in its raw power posing challenges to all who pass this way, and also with timeless beauty dating back to the formation of some of the oldest rocks on earth. American Indian petroglyphs and ruins, green ledges of dripping water at Vasey's Paradise, tributary waterfalls, and narrow fluted side canyons are all enticements to this unforgettable place.

Launching from Lee's Ferry, 16 miles below Glen Canyon Dam, and drifting into the Grand Canyon's incomparable cleft in the Colorado Plateau, boaters admire the rusty-red walls rising up and up. The flow funnels to powerful flumes of blue-green water—once consistently brown with silt, which is now trapped upstream in the bottom of Powell Reservoir. Meanwhile the beauty of the desert canyon grows more overwhelming by the mile and by the day. Perhaps the most astonishing element of the whole experience is that of scale. Everything is outlandishly large: the walls, the flow, the rapids, and the maze of tributary incisions into a plateau that covers much of the American Southwest.

Some sixty-seven major rapids build in crescendos to a pair of outsized drops: Crystal Rapid and Lava Falls. Many rapids can and should be

Lava Falls is the big rapid of the Grand Canyon. The preferred route lies to the right of this raft's line in the Colorado, whose waters are reddened to a bizarre extent by midsummer flooding of upstream tributaries.

OPPOSITE: An evening rainbow arcs across the Grand Canyon above Unkar Rapid.

scouted. The heavy volume requires frequent use of the "downriver ferry," accomplished by pointing the front of the raft downriver at either a left or right angle and rowing hard. This contrasts to the rafter's usual upriver ferry, which on the Colorado loses too much distance to the force of the flow. Setting up correctly at the top of rapids is essential, as attempts to significantly change position in mid-descent are futile.

Glen Canyon Dam releases typically vary in summer from 5,000 to 7,000 cfs and in springtime from 8,000 to 14,000 cfs, all requiring boaters to beware of a "tidal" effect when tying up boats.

The full trip is 280 miles from Lee's Ferry to Pearce Ferry in Lake Mead (in the past, a full reservoir required a 40-mile flatwater tow to the takeout, but the reservoir, for now, has receded

owing to persistent drought). A shorter trip runs 226 miles to Diamond Creek.

Nonmotorized expeditions need two weeks or so and should be undertaken only by groups of accomplished boaters or with a professional outfitter. Noncommercial trips require a permit chosen by lottery. Permits are usually available in December and January, when cold weather, frigid water temperatures, and perpetual canyon shade test the hardiest of boaters. From March to November the chances of securing a permit on any given year are less than ten percent, decreasing greatly in summer (see complex rules and procedures online).

The way most people join a noncommercial trip is by invitation of the person who has been awarded a permit. Support for private trips is

available from businesses in Flagstaff that provide boats, gear, food, and shuttles, making this expedition's formidable logistics easier.

Commercial trips are more readily scheduled, as, under Park Service rules, outfitters receive eighty-five percent of the permitted slots in summer months. Trips now cost $5,000 or so. Shorter motorized options are somewhat less expensive—but motorized, with large rafts.

Up until 1968 the Bureau of Reclamation proposed two dams here, and the battle over them became a landmark campaign in America's emerging environmental movement. President Lyndon B. Johnson declared the upstream portion, Marble Canyon, a national monument. In 1975 this was rolled into an enlarged Grand Canyon National Park, but external threats remain.

In recent years, sprawling resorts, an aerial tram, and uranium mining adjacent to the park have all imperiled this venerable place. Meanwhile the construction and operation of Glen Canyon Dam, directly upstream, has degraded the river, including severe erosion of beaches. Dam-induced changes in the temperature and flow of water have caused local extinction of native fish once thriving in warmer, naturally silty water, while exotic species of carp and trout thrive.

For those who are not able to undertake this extraordinary trip, tantalizing views are seen from Grand Canyon National Park's South Rim and from trails that descend a vertical mile to the water. For those who get to board a raft and go, it's the trip of a lifetime.

Tumultuous Granite Rapid looks small from this perch below the South Rim of the Grand Canyon.

SAN JUAN RIVER | Utah

SOUTHWEST

LENGTH: 27 to 103 miles

WHITEWATER: Class 2-3

SEASON: April to September; May to June for optimum flows and weather

GAUGE: Bluff

PERMIT: yes, and limited, especially early in the season

CAMPING: yes

OUTFITTERS: guided trips, rental rafts and kayaks

HIGHLIGHTS: desert canyon, hiking, pictographs, multiday Class 2-3 boating

Rapids of the San Juan make for an excellent, easy raft trip or a lively run by kayakers or skilled canoeists. Below Mexican Hat, these rafts coast through the glow of evening light in one of the West's greatest canyons.

This desert river blends lively but unintimidating rapids with a spectacular canyon, a rich display of ancient rock art and ruins, and great ledge walks or side-canyon hiking.

For bona fide desert lovers, the San Juan is the real deal. Warm in spring, intensely hot in summer, harshly rugged throughout, and spare of green, it flows muddy with corrosive erosion and it thickens to bizarre red opacity during the July to August flash-flood season. This may be the warmest water you're ever likely to paddle, and summer heat makes frequent swims mandatory. Nights are enchantingly balmy in their soft, carefree, star-spangled warmth.

Lacking the elegant cottonwood bottoms of the Green River's Desolation Canyon, the clear water of the dam-controlled Grand Canyon, or the frigid early season of the Owyhee, the San Juan perhaps best describes the archetypal desert river of the West. Below Bluff, the Butler Wash rock art panels and nearby River House ruins are among the finest remnants of pre-Pueblo southwestern culture in America. This is also the best facsimile of the Grand Canyon, offering, say, seventy percent of the awesome scenery with only ten percent of the expenses, permit restrictions, and skill requirements.

Typical trips start at the BLM's Sand Island access near Bluff and run 27 miles to another access at Mexican Hat, then onward for another 57 miles through dramatic canyon wilderness to the remote Clay Hills access perched near backwaters of Glen Canyon Dam. This run includes the unique 20-mile entrenched windings of the Goosenecks, where Honaker Trail switchbacks up to the canyon rim. An optional 19 riffling miles with red-rock cliffs, rock art, and buggy but bird-filled riparian flats

OPPOSITE: While storm clouds darken in the background, a silt-laden wave breaks in front of the raft midway through the San Juan's Gooseneck bends downstream from Mexican Hat.

In the hot, parched, and rugged canyon, a desert bighorn sheep ventures down to the San Juan's shoreline to drink and browse upstream from the river's final takeout at Clay Hills.

Deep within the canyons of the lower San Juan, Ann Vileisis cooks dinner aboard the raft as clouds darken with heat-quenching moisture wafting north from the Gulf of Mexico in late summer.

OPPOSITE: Opaque with sediment flushed by recent flash floods, the San Juan foams over boulders that previous high flows have rolled down tributaries and deposited in the main channel at Twin Canyons.

can be added to the beginning of the float by driving upriver from Bluff to the BLM's Montezuma Creek put-in, for a total expedition of 103 miles.

Expect few trees for shade, but rather rock walls, endless sandstone curiosities, and intricate side canyons with opportunities to explore on foot, especially at Grand Gulch. The takeout is gruesome in summer heat and a sticky mud-mired shoreline, and the rattling access road is corrugated by dozens of intermittent washes—nothing for the faint of heart—but it's all worth the effort.

With its rapids, wave trains, and rocks to avoid, the San Juan appeals to experienced canoeists, kayakers of developing skill levels, and capable families in rafts. In a canoe loaded with camping gear, four or more of the rapids (Eight Foot, Gypsum Creek, Ross, and Government) are especially challenging, requiring scouting and optional rocky portages; rafts are the preferred craft for most boaters.

One of the siltiest rivers in America, even the foam is brown or strangely red, making pourovers cryptic just to see. In the lower 10 miles, boaters additionally confront silt buildup from the distant Glen Canyon Dam. This calls for crucial reading of subtle braiding to avoid shallows and laborious dragging of boats that can threaten to get firmly stuck.

On the south side, the Navajo Nation requires permits for hiking or camping through most of the trip's length. The north side is mostly BLM land with good campsites and attractive ledges available. In addition to the boating permit, campsite reservations are required for the lower 20 miles.

March is cold but doable for prepared travelers. April is cool, but springtime begins to break. May is prime if permits are available and water levels aren't too pushy for personal skill levels. June and July are hot with normally adequate flows. In late summer, permits are easier to get. Flows then may dip too low for rafts, though summer monsoon rains often begin in mid-July, bumping levels up, moderating the heat with cloudiness, and erratically triggering spectacular flash floods. Beware of camping near the tempting waterline or at tributary mouths. If rainfall fails in late summer, levels may drop too low for all craft.

Another tributary to the lower Colorado, the Salt River in central Arizona has Class 4 rapids through a scenic wilderness canyon, with flows usually limited to March and April. Forest Service permits are required.

RIO GRANDE | New Mexico

LENGTH: 5 to 79 miles, mostly run as day trips

WHITEWATER: Class 2–5

SEASON: spring, summer; Taos Box is usually too low by July

GAUGE: Taos Junction Bridge

PERMIT: yes, for some sections, from the BLM in Taos

CAMPING: mostly at campgrounds on road-accessible sections

OUTFITTERS: guided trips

HIGHLIGHTS: whitewater, canyon scenery, geology

America's fifth-longest river (though small in volume of flow), the 1,885-mile Rio Grande, begins in fir forests of Colorado, where headwaters include a Class 4 kayaking run and a 12-mile Class 2 reach at Wagon Wheel Gap, upstream from the South Fork. After flowing into New Mexico, the river enters some of the most extreme desert canyons in America.

As the Southwest's premier one-day trip for intense whitewater, the Rio Grande through Taos Box plunges over multiple lava ledges and through cluttered remains of rockslides. From the plateau, the 800-foot canyon walls are so abrupt that the cleft is not even evident until you nearly reach the rim. For an easy view, stroll across the 667-foot-tall Route 64 bridge northwest of Taos—not for the acrophobic—and walk downriver from there on a West Rim trail.

The famous cliff-bound Taos Box runs 16 miles, where the excitement and chill of whitewater blasting through such a narrow space astonishes. Few rivers have such extreme depth-to-width ratios. The action includes a one-story plunge over Powerline Rapid, portaged at low flows. High springtime waters create a chaos of muddy foam. Most rafting here is done in late spring and until July. Paddle-rafts are suited for confronting the multitude of sharp rocks, frowning keeper holes, and sudden mandatory moves. Commercial trips are best for all but seasoned experts. The run begins at Dunn Bridge, northwest of Taos; take out at Taos Junction Bridge, Highway 570 northeast of Pilar.

Both above and below Taos Box, New Mexico's Rio Grande offers more:

→ Ute Mountain Run: This is New Mexico's uppermost reach, 24 miles, Class 2, closed until July for raptor nesting, runnable

The Lower Taos Box of the Rio Grande is the most challenging whitewater day trip in the Southwest. High on the canyon wall, a juniper tree catches morning light.

The enchanting Middle Box of the Rio Grande begins at the mouth of the Red River and is reached by a 2-mile trail in Rio Grande del Norte National Monument.

OPPOSITE: The monsoon season from mid-July through August can bring intense afternoon rainstorms, like the one soaking rafters here in the Middle Box.

with autumn rains from September to November on a minimum of 200 cfs. Not for everyone, the takeout requires a steep three-quarter-mile hike. Call the BLM in Taos for reservations.

➤ Razorblades, Upper Box, and La Junta sections: These 22 miles of Class 3–5 are for expert kayakers only and have steep trails for access. Reserve with the BLM.

➤ Middle Box: Eight miles of Class 3+ are spectacular and wild; put in with a 1-mile trail descent to the mouth of the Red River.

➤ Taos Box: These 16 miles with Class 4 rapids run from Dunn Bridge to Taos Junction Bridge; see narrative above.

➤ Taos Junction Bridge (Highway 570) to Quartzite ramp off Highway 68, half a mile below Pilar: Six miles of Class 2 include a passable rock dam at Pilar, with easy access, runnable all summer. Paralleled by a paved road serving only recreational traffic, this is one of the finest road-accessible river recreation corridors in the Southwest with multiple campgrounds and accesses to Class 1–2 water.

→ Pilar Racecourse: Five miles from the Quartzite ramp to the County Line ramp flow along Highway 68. This Class 3–4 water with easy access is heavily used all summer.

→ Bosque: Seven miles of Class 1–2 continue from the County Line ramp to Embudo Bridge, with road frontage and houses but also short undeveloped sections, runnable all summer.

Most Rio Grande paddlers take day trips and stay at campgrounds. Far Flung Adventures offers a three-day, 40-mile upper river trip, plus the full suite of day trips, including the Middle Box where horses pack in the rafts.

All but the lower 6 miles discussed here are protected as one of the first National Wild and Scenic Rivers; however, reaches both above and below are heavily affected by diversions. Native sturgeon, eel, redhorse, and four species of smaller fish are locally extinct while the silvery minnow is endangered. Amigos Bravos works for protection of this river.

A northern New Mexico tributary to the Rio Grande, the Rio Chama also makes for a colorfully picturesque Class 2–3 trip for 35 miles between El Vado Dam and Abiquiu Reservoir; a BLM permit is required. It is best run in spring at 1,000 cfs, but it is runnable by kayaks and canoes on unpredictable dam releases down to 200 cfs on summer weekdays and by larger craft on 600 cfs releases on summer weekends.

The Rio Grande's Racecourse section offers 5 miles of whitewater and spectacular mountain views while a road alongside provides easy access.

RIO GRANDE | Texas

LENGTH: 10 to 298 miles

WHITEWATER: Class 2-3

SEASON: late winter, spring, fall

GAUGE: Johnson's Ranch

PERMIT: yes, no limit

CAMPING: yes

OUTFITTERS: guided trips, rental canoes

HIGHLIGHTS: long remote trip, desert wilderness, deep canyon, U.S.-Mexico border

Benefiting from summer rain showers, vegetation of the Chihuahuan Desert thrives along the Rio Grande.

For river runners seeking a middle or late winter escape, and ready for the edginess of the Mexican border, this river runs through some of the most spectacular vertical wall desert canyons on the continent.

Drifting here can continue for days or weeks through miniature versions of the Grand Canyon. But they don't seem miniature because the scale of river width to canyon depth is so extreme. Walls climb 1,000 feet in narrow slots. Currents emerge from inner sanctums of split-apart mountains, wind through intervening valleys, and then pass again through a crack in the wall of a great escarpment to enter yet another canyon.

Hikes can be taken up tributaries to rims with views overlooking harsh drylands. This is America's only river trip in the Chihuahuan Desert, known for diverse flora benefiting from both winter rain and autumn monsoons. Riffles accelerate to moderate rapids with a few larger drops that canoeists portage.

Upriver, the Rio Grande of southern New Mexico has been totally diverted below Elephant Butte Dam, and then the Texas portion of the river—1,254 miles along the international border—is resupplied by the dam-controlled Rio Conchos of Mexico. From the Conchos's mouth near Presidio, the Rio Grande runs dam-free to Amistad Reservoir. Trips span 129 miles through Big Bend National Park, followed by the Lower Canyons to Dryden Crossing—altogether 298 miles of canoeing extravaganza.

However, borderland issues deserve full disclosure here. Consider the extreme remoteness. Even if you happen to be driving across the 900-mile width of Texas on its southernmost interstate highway—which is unlikely—the river still lies

160 miles off your route. Access roads can be rough and some are private and impassible in rain. Vehicles should not be left near the river; use professional shuttle services that will safely keep your car and pick you up or deliver your rig on schedule. Virtually all the water is muddy and polluted return flow from irrigated agriculture and Mexican cities. Exotic reeds grow impenetrably on many floodplains, except that on the Mexican side, most are trampled and denuded by feral cows and horses. Boaters might consider calling Big Bend National Park officials to inquire if any safety issues are relevant to the border area. Drinking water should be carried, though some springs percolate into the Lower Canyons. And beware of rattlesnakes.

All that said, the borderland Rio Grande is a Wild West journey unlike any other. The river can be divided into seven shorter trips:

- Colorado Canyon: Downstream from Presidio, this 21-mile float includes 8-mile-long Colorado Canyon with takeout at Lajitas, Class 2–3.
- Santa Elena Canyon: This popular day trip can run 20 miles, from Lajitas to the canyon mouth. For 7 miles the walls of an inner gorge rise to 1,500 feet. Strong canoeing skills are needed at Rock Slide Rapid. Here and below, Big Bend National Park requires permits.
- Next section: This 40-mile interval of bluffs and drylands is rarely paddled.
- Mariscal Canyon: Ten popular Big Bend miles extend from Talley to Solis Landing, including Mariscal Canyon, 6 miles long with 1,400-foot walls, Class 2–3.

→ San Vicente and Hot Springs Canyons: Nineteen miles run from Solis Landing to Rio Grande Village, Class 2.

→ Boquillas Canyon: Thirty-three miles run from Rio Grande Village to La Linda, Class 2. This is the second-most popular reach, with easier rapids.

→ Lower Canyons: Downstream from the national park, 83 miles continue from La Linda to Dryden Crossing, or 119 miles in all to Foster's Ranch (permission required). Rapids include several portages for canoes. Little access here makes this one of the wildest desert trips in America. Boaters may encounter Mexicans collecting candelilla for commercial sale, squatters living along the south shore and setting lines for catfish, cowboys nominally tending cattle, and perhaps a few other floaters. But more likely you will see no one.

This is the United States' southernmost river, possibly balmy even in January, though there's no guarantee of that, and winter nights often dip below freezing. Cold snaps can occur through March, but springtime is generally ideal. Summer is wickedly hot and water quality may be poor. Cooler late-season trips benefit from monsoon rains.

Boquillas Canyon of the Rio Grande is one of several at the border of Texas and Mexico. A variety of day trips or extended expeditions tour the edge of Big Bend National Park and continue below it.

CALIFORNIA

The Golden State is a rivers empire with waters streaming off gleaming peaks of the Sierra Nevada and from the biologically rich woodlands of the mountainous north.

In a class by themselves, rivers of the Sierra Nevada flow from consolidated snowpacks twelve feet deep. Streams on the west side of these mountains tumble through a wonderland of saw-toothed peaks, granite domes, and white bedrock slabs down to pine forests and sunny oak savanna. East-slope rivers fall from the steep seismic escarpment to the Great Basin Desert with its scent of sage. No other region displays the brilliance of light and color, the clarity of water, the numbers and steepness of rapids, and the accessibility for trips of one to three days. From north to south, on the wetter Pacific slope alone, the Feather, Yuba, American, Mokelumne, Stanislaus, Tuolumne, Merced, San Joaquin, Kings, Kaweah, and Kern are all magnificent. Because these streams are also blocked by dams, river trips are short, but adventures can be launched throughout.

The North Fork Kern lunges through a whitewater wilderness unlike any other. The Kings has the greatest undammed vertical drop in America, and 9 miles through picturesque oak savanna are a rollicking whitewater run. The Merced drifts like an idyll in waterfall-ringed Yosemite Valley and then churns through public land below. The Tuolumne challenges boaters with elegant rapids in a foothills canyon. The American River's South Fork is one of the most popular whitewater runs in the United States. The Mokelumne has sweet early season day trips, and the North and South Yuba have excellent short whitewater slaloms for advanced kayakers in springtime.

Northern California and the south coast of Oregon have the nation's greatest concentration of excellent wild rivers. In fact, the network of waterways there is nothing *but* great wild or semiwild rivers. They start with the Eel, through redwood corridors, and continue northward through the Klamath and Smith River basins and onward into Oregon for a continuous north-south sweep of 250 miles. The Smith and its forks have outstanding whitewater, and the Klamath offers the longest river trip on the West Coast—dam-free, with hundreds of rapids and one portage—for nearly 200 miles to the ocean.

With California's incline from highcountry to sea level and its geographic sweep from rain forests moderated by temperate Pacific storms to southern drylands and deserts, the seasons of river running span spring through fall and include rainy wintertime for savvy boaters on the coastal rivers of the north.

KERN RIVER, NORTH FORK | California

LENGTH: 17 miles, plus lower reaches

WHITEWATER: Class 5

SEASON: late spring, early summer

GAUGE: Fairview Dam

PERMIT: yes

CAMPING: yes

OUTFITTERS: guided trips

HIGHLIGHTS: intense whitewater, wilderness camping, Sierra Nevada scenery

PREVIOUS SPREAD: California has an incomparable variety of rivers from granite peaks of the Sierra Nevada, deep forests of the north, and rugged terrain of the Coast Ranges. With crystal clear waters, the North Fork of the Smith is among the state's wildest rivers with challenging rafting on high runoff after winter storms.

In early light of daybreak, the North Fork Kern plunges over ledges of granite in its southbound course between high paralleling ridges of the southern Sierra Nevada.

The North Fork (upper) Kern makes a stunning descent from the western flanks of Mount Whitney—the highest peak in forty-nine states—to hot foothills of the southern Sierra Nevada, with extraordinary whitewater along the way. Steep, difficult, and alluring, this wilderness run seems longer than its 17 miles. In their book *California Whitewater*, Jim Cassady and Fryar Calhoun called it "one of the finest stretches of expert whitewater on earth."

Not for the faint of heart, the Forks of the Kern reach challenges expert kayakers and rafters at five Class 5 rapids plus a whirlwind of lesser drops. Anyone who is not fully competent here should go with an outfitter; even then boaters will be roused with intense paddling or, at times, an iron grip simply to stay in the boat.

The Kern is the closest regularly run whitewater to Los Angeles. But after the drive, this trip requires a 2-mile hike with backpacks or a kayak over the shoulder. Horse packers can be arranged to carry rafts for launching at the confluence of the Little Kern and North Fork. Unlike most other runs in California, this one lies in mountain country at 4,680 feet with views not to foothills, oaks, and chaparral, but to granite domes, jagged cliffs, and conifers deep in snow until hot weather arrives.

Eighty major rapids explode through the early summer boating season. Intense demands come at mile 11 with Vortex Rapid. West Wall rates Class 5 for a quarter mile with an eight-foot pitch at the bottom. At Carson Falls a random hydraulic can flip any raft; some boaters portage. The takeout comes shortly after at Johnsondale Bridge.

Kayakers hustle here as a day trip, but the unforgettable splendor is best savored as a two- or three-day excursion. Along with the Tuolumne, this is one of few rivers from the water-rich slopes of the Sierra Nevada that's boatable for multiday length without dams. The water often drops too low for rafts by mid-July. For permits, call the Forest Service at Lake Isabella Visitor Center of Sequoia National Forest.

North Fork boating continues below the low-head Fairview Dam with more Class 3–5 rapids that get heavy use from the paved road alongside. Below Isabella Reservoir, the main-stem Kern resumes with Class 4 whitewater, while the lower main stem is widely recognized as a nonboating chain of waterfalls and death-trap boulders along Highway 178 east of Bakersfield.

Another multiday California wilderness trip with astounding beauty and comparably intense whitewater for expert paddlers is the Middle Fork Feather, at the northern end of the Sierra Nevada.

Among many excellent rivers that cascade from incomparable highcountry of the Sierra Nevada, the North Fork Kern is exceptional with Class 4-5 rapids.

TUOLUMNE RIVER | California

LENGTH: 18 miles, plus the Cherry Creek run of 9 miles

WHITEWATER: Class 4-5

SEASON: spring, summer

GAUGE: Meral's Pool

PERMIT: yes, and limited

CAMPING: yes

OUTFITTERS: guided trips

HIGHLIGHTS: premier whitewater run, wilderness

The "T" is one of America's most revered whitewater destinations. This basin forms the northern portion of Yosemite National Park, where headwaters at Tuolumne Meadows draw millions to highcountry heights of the Sierra Nevada. Downstream, the Grand Canyon of the Tuolumne offers an unmatched riverfront trail replete with waterfalls, followed by Hetch Hetchy Reservoir.

About 30 miles below that dam, rafters and kayakers embark at Meral's Pool on a Class 4–5 run to Don Pedro Reservoir, best with one or two nights of camping, but also done in one day.

The 2,000-foot-deep canyon features cliffs, ponderosa pines, oak savanna, and chaparral. Steep drops with powerful hydraulics, undercut rocks, and highly technical maneuvering characterize Class 4 rapids. A greater challenge is the steeply downward escalator of Clavey Falls, which leads to a monster hole. The takeout for this otherwise stellar run can involve paddling a mile or more in Don Pedro Reservoir.

Spring and early summer bring hazardously high water until the snowpack declines in July. Summers are hot, making the Tuolumne's constant splash a welcome relief. Dam controlled, the river can often be run into autumn, with 1,000 cfs nearing the low limit for rafts. Permits are required and rationed; call Groveland Ranger Station of Stanislaus National Forest.

Above that popular reach of the Tuolumne, the Cherry Creek run begins on a dam-controlled tributary, which in a mile enters the Tuolumne and a Class 5 lineup of boulder-stop drops—the most challenging regularly run commercial raft trip in the West, suited only for skilled paddlers, even in a professionally guided raft.

Upstream on the Tuolumne at San Francisco's Hetch Hetchy dam site, pioneering preservationist John Muir, in the early 1900s, waged his most famous battle, seeking to spare from damming the only valley comparable to nearby Yosemite. The river and Hetch Hetchy Valley were impounded, but Muir's struggle launched the modern movement to protect America's most outstanding streams from damming. Other efforts to impound and divert the river were resisted by the Tuolumne River Trust, and the mileage above Don Pedro Reservoir was designated a National Wild and Scenic River in 1984. Further defense and restoration work by the trust continues.

In a reprieve from its lineup of technical rapids, the Tuolumne near Indian Creek eases for a placid interlude in its descent west of Yosemite National Park.

FOLLOWING SPREAD: The Tuolumne River excels with some of the finest whitewater that is regularly run in the West. Here Clavey Falls keeps rowers on guard with its staircase entrance and angry midriver hole.

AMERICAN RIVER, SOUTH FORK | California

LENGTH: 6 or 10 miles in two sections

WHITEWATER: Class 3-4

SEASON: all year

GAUGE: Chili Bar

PERMIT: yes, but not limited, from El Dorado County Parks Department

CAMPING: commercial campgrounds plus a few remote sites; call BLM Mother Lode Field Office for permits

OUTFITTERS: guided trips, rental rafts

HIGHLIGHTS: whitewater day trips, festive social boating atmosphere

Troublemaker is the big rapid of the South Fork American upstream of Coloma. This river of the Sierra Nevada foothills is one of the most popular whitewater streams in the West.

Two day trips make the American one of the most floated whitewater rivers in the nation—130,000 people per year. Rapids excite kayakers and rafters from start to finish on both these runs.

The South Fork plays prominently in the heritage and culture of whitewater running in California with bustling businesses in private boating, outfitted trips, kayak schools, shuttle services, campgrounds, and support facilities centered at Coloma, between the two popular sections.

Summer days are hot in these foothills; spring and fall are glorious. Even in winter, dry-suited paddlers find pleasant days with year-round flows guaranteed by Sierra Nevada snowpacks, plus upstream reservoirs that even out runoff. Adequate flows were established after hard-earned negotiations by local outfitter and river conservation champion Bill Center, who also happened to have saved these stellar runs from dam and diversion proposals back in the 1970s.

Outfitted trips are an industry here, and the river draws thousands of independent paddlers from San Francisco, Sacramento, and beyond. At 3,000 cfs, the American becomes a significant big-water challenge. At low flows it's a top run for expert canoeists. Discriminating boaters will want to avoid summer weekends, which are mobbed and require waiting time above major rapids.

The upper run, from Chili Bar Dam to Coloma, climaxes near the end with Class 4 Troublemaker Rapid. From the takeout in Sutter's Mill, where the California Gold Rush began, 4 miles of Class 2 water are followed by the South Fork Gorge for another 10 miles, packed with whitewater,

including a beautifully foaming Class 4 rapid misnamed Satan's Cesspool.

Overnighting is limited to commercial campgrounds, such as Camp Lotus at the head of the gorge run, and at a few Bureau of Land Management (BLM) sites. The South Fork is thus a hybrid experience of two whitewater days with car camping between. At last notice, shuttle service by bus was available through the River Store near Coloma.

Within a few hours' drive of Northern California population centers, the South Fork is many people's entry point for whitewater paddling, whether as independent kayakers and rafters or with outfitters.

Above Chili Bar, the South Fork's Kyburz Run and a few others challenge Class 4–5 kayakers in spring and early summer, and the nearby North Fork American promises Class 4–5 whitewater in several reaches. Below Folsom Dam, the main-stem American accommodates masses of Class 1–2 floaters through Sacramento in one of the nation's most extensive and popular urban greenways.

The South Fork American speeds toward the village and historic site of Coloma.

KLAMATH RIVER | California

LENGTH: 4 to 193 miles, with many access points

WHITEWATER: Class 2-4, with one portage by vehicle

SEASON: spring, summer, fall

GAUGE: Iron Gate, Happy Camp

PERMIT: no

CAMPING: yes

OUTFITTERS: guided trips for several reaches

HIGHLIGHTS: West Coast's longest semiwild trip, mostly moderate whitewater, wildlife

A smooth tongue of water funnels into Bluff Creek Rapid in the lower Klamath.

On the West Coast south of Canada, the Klamath is the third-largest river and, among major basins, it has the most intact forests and undammed mileage.

Below five dams straddling the Oregon border, the Klamath flows free for 193 miles to the Pacific—all boatable except for a highway portage midway at Ishi Pishi Falls. With a few major rapids and hundreds of minor ones, this is the longest whitewater trip on the West Coast. Highway 96 deters boaters seeking wilderness but is mostly perched high or set back, and it interferes little with appreciation of this river. Homes are scattered in some sections, but most frontage is forested.

At epidemic concentrations in Oregon's headwater sources of shallow lakes, reservoirs, and return irrigation ditches, a polluting blue-green algae degrades Klamath water as the river crosses into California, though the problem is not enough to impair river travel, and cold tributaries improve water quality as the river pushes toward the Pacific.

The Klamath slips through Class 2 rapids with an occasional Class 3 and frequent access points for 64 delightful miles from Iron Gate Dam to Fort Goff. Below there, 3 miles of Class 3 are followed by 16 miles of Class 1 to Happy Camp. Then Class 3 is mixed with easier water for 36 miles. None of the Klamath gets heavy use, but this whitewater section, with guided trips, sees the most.

Upstream of Somes Bar, the Green Riffle access is a mandatory takeout above the long Class 5 plunge of Ishi Pishi Falls, also revered as a sacred site by local American Indians. Below there, a westside launch leads directly to The Ikes—a Class 3–4+ chain of hydraulics and waves mounding like haystacks in springtime, with the first hole likely to flip rafts at 15,000 cfs or perhaps less. These are followed by 18 miles of Class 2–3 to the Trinity River.

The lower Klamath is mostly gentle water for 37 miles through the Yurok Reservation, where camping is discouraged, though possible on scattered federal parcels or with permission and a fee. Here the Klamath completes its transformation from a river that begins on the dry eastern slopes of the Cascades and passes through the Coast Range to emerge in fog and oceanic chill that nourishes recovering redwoods. A final takeout at Requa perches just above the Pacific surf.

From mid-July to late August, Karuk Indians hold ceremonies along the river between Wingate Bar (10 miles below Happy Camp) and Orleans; avoid prescribed sites even in passing. Call Klamath National Forest in Happy Camp for annual details.

During winter the Klamath floods torrentially, and springtime promises formidable water. By July levels decline but remain powerful. Even in drought years, strong boatable flows persist with 5,000 cfs through a balmy autumn. Moderate

On the Klamath River downstream of Interstate 5, sunbeams pierce an ominously darkening sky as a thunderstorm approaches (top left). Within a short walk of the river, hikers inch their way along a ledge leading to twin waterfalls on Ukonom Creek, a Klamath tributary 20 miles downstream from Happy Camp. In basins with forests protected from clearcutting, feeder streams, such as this one, deliver fresh water to the main-stem Klamath where the cool runoff is needed to sustain salmon and steelhead (bottom left).

OPPOSITE: The Klamath is one of few major rivers on the West Coast south of Canada lacking jetties or obstructions at its ocean outlet. During low flows, river runners can go nearly to the surf, beaching on the barrier bar and then returning to a takeout on the north side.

flows are run in rafts, dories, and kayaks, and at lower levels, expert canoeists can sneak around most of the big-volume drops.

Two Klamath tributaries also make for great river trips. Joining the lower Klamath, the Trinity offers 100 miles of Class 2–4 boating with multiple accesses, plus the Class 5 Burnt Ranch Gorge. The Salmon River ("Cal Salmon") is the West Coast's superlative Class 5 day trip as it careens toward the Klamath near Somes Bar.

The full length of California's Klamath is an underrated gem that will benefit from restoration underway to eliminate four upper river dams, to cool warm water with recovering forests and restored wetlands, and to ensure the release of adequate flow from a Trinity River dam where water is diverted to central California farms.

Savage Rapids is one among hundreds of Class 2-3 drops in the Klamath River through its 193-mile descent from Iron Gate Dam in northeastern California to the Pacific—all runnable except for portage of Ishi Pishi Falls by vehicle.

PACIFIC NORTHWEST

By any measure a land of rivers, the streams of the Pacific Northwest are many and varied through rain forests of the Coast Range, conifer groves of the Cascade Mountains, and dry terrain east of the high peaks. With sources in the Cascade Mountains of the interior Northwest and then completely transecting the Coast Range, the Rogue and Umpqua Rivers of southern Oregon tour the most diverse forests in the West; more species of conifers thrive there than anywhere else on earth. The Rogue is world renowned for its four-day wilderness sojourn, fish, frequent rapids, and tempting campsites. The Umpqua crosses tamer terrain, but its milder rapids and mostly undeveloped shores make it one of America's great canoe trips for 100 miles.

A suite of Cascade Mountain rivers incise that snowcapped volcanic range strung down the center of Oregon, where the forks of the Willamette, McKenzie, Santiam, and Clackamas all offer excellent day trips. These feed the Willamette in its gentle journey northward. East of the Cascades, the Deschutes, John Day, Grande Ronde, Owyhee, and Snake cut basalt canyons as memorable passages through the Northwest's own iteration of the Great American Desert. Washington appeals with waterfall descents into the Columbia Gorge, including several on the White Salmon River. Snowmelt from the Cascade Mountains flows summerlong in the Skagit and other streams, while a fabulous radial splay of free-flowing wonders plunge from the heights of the Olympic Mountains. Finally, east-slope waters, such as the Yakima, cross colorful dryland terrain of the Columbia's interior basin.

In the coastal region, serious boaters with drysuits are not deterred by cold winter rains. Rainy and snowy winter weather begins to warm in April when the high flows of the low-elevation rivers subside and the snowmelt torrents from the Cascades increase. Then in summer the waters clear to blue-green depths. Some streams continue flowing through a delectable autumn until winter rains advance from the Pacific again.

ROGUE RIVER | Oregon

LENGTH: 34 to 157 miles

WHITEWATER: Class 2-4

SEASON: spring, summer, fall

GAUGE: Grants Pass, Agness (below Wild Rogue run)

PERMIT: yes, limited in number from May 15 to October 15

CAMPING: yes

OUTFITTERS: guided trips

HIGHLIGHTS: whitewater, camping, fishing, long season, family trips with outfitters or for experienced rafters

PREVIOUS SPREAD: A classic river of the Northwest, the Rogue speeds over bedrock below Grave Creek, where most whitewater trips on this popular stream begin. Flowing from Cascade Mountain sources to the Pacific, the river cuts directly across the grain of Oregon's Coast Range uplift.

At Mule Creek Canyon, the Rogue boils through a mile-long slot in bedrock, sometimes only twenty feet wide.

The Rogue is the great multiday river trip of the Northwest, and travels on it run deep in the regional lore of river running and fishing dating to Zane Grey novels. Long before the modern era of whitewater boating, western guides rowed driftboats here with clients casting for salmon and steelhead—trophy fish that still attract anglers.

With an abundance of Class 3 rapids and a few larger ones, and with Edenic campsites, intoxicating weather, a season lingering deep into autumn, plus adequate flows as dependable as any, this is a favorite four-day trip.

The standard outing starts at Grave Creek, 34 miles downstream from Grants Pass, and runs another 34 miles with roadless riverfront to Foster Bar east of Gold Beach. Immediately below the put-in, Grave Creek Rapid and Falls are sudden drops, followed in 2 miles by the horizon line of Rainie Falls. Most boaters sneak through a far-right rocky passage blasted out decades ago to help salmon swimming upstream and driftboats headed downstream. After a two-day menu of intricate rapids, Mule Creek Canyon's unique mile-long crevice measures barely twenty feet wide in places. Then comes Blossom Bar Rapid—left-side entry followed by an immediate and mandatory eddy tuck to the right to avoid a gallery of pinning rocks bristling from the left shore.

This run can be enhanced by starting 7 miles farther up at the Galice ramp or nearby put-ins. Better—though few do it for the gentler water involved—start at Grants Pass for a 68-mile trip.

And for those seeking a major expedition, the Rogue trip can be extended up to Lost Creek Dam. From there, an otherwise easy 37 miles is punctuated by two cryptic and gnarly Class 4 rapids above the town of Gold Hill. These can be avoided by

The Rogue is a classic western river trip. A wild 34-mile canyon draws boaters nationwide to its extravaganza of Class 3-4 whitewater, alluring campsites, and salmon fishing. Here, below Blossom Bar Rapid, the lower Rogue pushes seaward.

taking out 32 miles below the dam at Fishers Ferry or by putting in 5 miles lower at Gold Hill, which is followed by 19 more miles of Class 1–2 riffles through the Interstate 5 corridor. At Grants Pass the Rogue drops into wilder terrain again with moderate rapids and occasional campsites down to the Grave Creek ramp and usual Wild Rogue put-in.

Likewise, downstream from the wild section, the lower Rogue flows another 33 miles to sea at Gold Beach through the emerald heart of the Coast Range. Though heavily cruised by jet boats, and with stiff afternoon headwinds, the lower river offers one of the West Coast's finest overnight trips with relatively easy rapids and spacious gravel bars. Combined, the mileage from Lost Creek to the ocean is one of the longest dam-free lengths of river on the Pacific coast.

Boating the Rogue's full 157 free-flowing miles is possible because three obsolete dams were

removed between 2008 and 2010. This enabled salmon to resume their ancient spawning run to upper tributaries.

The Rogue was one of the original National Wild and Scenic Rivers designated in 1968 and soon became a model with permit procedures, access development, and maintenance that helped shape river management elsewhere. Continuing watershed restoration and protection are aimed at restoring legendary runs of salmon and steelhead.

For the terrestrial, the Wild Rogue below Grave Creek is also served by a 40-mile north-bank trail. Beware of poison oak, and take bear precautions with food storage.

The Rogue's largest tributary, the Illinois River, is an awesome whitewater destination in its own right. Class 4–5 rapids make this river a favorite of advanced boaters. Its season is limited to springtime, preferably May, on flows of 1,500 cfs or so. Watch the weather forecast; the Illinois spikes insanely with rainstorms.

The Rogue's wild reach is a good choice for boaters, including families looking for an exciting trip but wanting to avoid the more challenging whitewater and longer outings or distant destinations required with some of the other great western rivers.

A commercial sportfishing guide holds a Chinook salmon that his client just caught in the middle Rogue below Grants Pass (top right). Ann Vileisis checks out a Class 3 rapid she just negotiated on the Rogue. Fine whitewater and a convenient wilderness trip await here within a one-day drive of both San Francisco and Portland (bottom right).

Blossom Bar Rapid requires a left-side entry with an immediate mandatory jog to the right. Here driftboat guides eddy hop through the lower half of the rapid.

UMPQUA RIVER | Oregon

LENGTH: 4 to 176 miles

WHITEWATER: Class 1–4; main stem is mostly Class 1–2

SEASON: spring, summer, fall

GAUGE: Elkton (lower), Tiller (South Umpqua), Winchester (North Umpqua)

PERMIT: no

CAMPING: yes

OUTFITTERS: guided trips on North Umpqua; fishing trips on the main stem

HIGHLIGHTS: long main-stem canoe trip, fishing, whitewater on North Umpqua

Driftboaters cast for smallmouth bass in summer and for salmon and steelhead in fall and winter along the main-stem Umpqua. This river offers an excellent extended trip with dozens of minor rapids and a few that are portaged by most canoeists.

Though virtually unknown as such, the main-stem Umpqua is not just a great Oregon canoe trip, but a great *American* canoe trip. From the North and South Umpqua confluence northwest of Roseburg to the ocean at Reedsport, 100 miles make a superb weeklong expedition for experienced canoeists. Hundreds of Class 2 rapids at low and medium flows, two Class 3 drops between the two Highway 138 bridges, and an easy portage at Sawyer's Rapid—10 miles below Elkton—mark this route. Not wilderness but rather a tour of rural Oregon, this is the West Coast's longest Pacific-bound canoe trip lacking dams, major levees, or multiple major rapids, with ample flows all summer and fall.

Starting at the main-stem source—River Forks Park northwest of Roseburg—public accesses occur every 6 to 10 miles with easy shuttles on paved roads. Fishing is outstanding with smallmouth bass through summer, plus Chinook salmon and steelhead in other seasons.

While roads parallel much of the Umpqua, sizable bends also loop away from highways and offer solitude. Unlike whitewater and wilderness rivers such as the nearby Rogue, few other boaters are encountered on this extended trip. Campsites can be found on scattered Bureau of Land Management (BLM) parcels, on bars, and on bedrock outcrops.

The main-stem trip can be lengthened in spring and early summer by launching on the South Umpqua as high as Tiller, adding 76 miles down to the North Umpqua confluence and then onward to Reedsport for a 176-mile expedition. The South Umpqua includes one Class 4 rapid, easily portaged, and a few Class 3 drops, but it's mostly easy Class 2 rapids. The route passes

through the Interstate 5 corridor, but even at small towns, paddling is pleasant for anyone wanting the full Umpqua experience and a long outing.

In contrast, the North Umpqua offers 31 miles of Class 3–4 whitewater in a pool-drop, action-packed descent. Clear water, deep forests, easy shuttles, and frequent access points are augmented with Forest Service campgrounds and a hiking and mountain biking trail of 79 miles to the head-waters, altogether making this tributary east of Roseburg one of the finest road-accessible river rec-reation corridors in the West. Below the hazardous Deadline Falls and Narrows upstream of Idleyld, the lower North Umpqua continues for 25 miles with Class 2 and a few steeper drops to backwaters of Winchester Dam near Roseburg.

OPPOSITE: The Umpqua crosses sandstone and basalt ledges at Elkton as the river nears a fjord-like conclusion at sea level.

Exploding waves in the South Umpqua River, 2 miles above Days Creek, are among only a few significant rapids on a 76-mile length of this Umpqua tributary. The main stem continues for another 100 miles and offers one of the longest canoe trips on the West Coast.

WILLAMETTE RIVER | Oregon

LENGTH: 5 to 189 miles

WHITEWATER: Class 1, Class 2 in upper reaches

SEASON: spring, summer, fall

GAUGE: Harrisburg (upper), Corvallis, Dexter for Middle Fork, Leaburg for McKenzie

PERMIT: no

CAMPING: yes

OUTFITTERS: guided trips or local rentals may be possible

HIGHLIGHTS: casual Class 1 paddling through agricultural Oregon, birds, fishing, campsites

The Willamette is the Huck Finn river of the Northwest with a week or two of Class 1 and 2 paddling from Dexter Dam on the Middle Fork or from the lower McKenzie River to a mandatory takeout at West Linn, near Portland and above Willamette Falls. Canoeists can drift, fish, bird-watch, and pause at towns along the way. Campsites, such as this one at the Luckiamute River, are part of the Willamette River Water Trail.

OPPOSITE: An aerial view of the Willamette's middle section shows its meandering passage through farms and woodlots.

For an extended Class 1 canoe voyage with few risks and the conveniences of civilization nearby, as well as riparian beauty through cottonwood forests, the Willamette is *the* West Coast destination. Access is easy and frequent through the agricultural and urban heartland of Oregon.

Something like the Delaware or Potomac of the East, this artery serves as the Huck Finn river of the Northwest. You can load a canoe with supplies, set yourself adrift, and spend a week or two gliding with the current, camping on gravel bars or shaded banks, fishing, reading books, and watch-ing birds. Tie up on shore to resupply at small towns where you can stroll the streets, or stop at parks with shady trails through woodlands. This is not the wilderness sojourn that marks other great American river trips, but rather one with perspective to the Northwest's riparian corridors, rural riverscapes, and waterfront towns.

For one of the West's longest canoe trips without dams, start on the McKenzie River at the base of Leaburg Dam. Lively Class 2 riffles continue 41 miles to the Willamette north of Eugene. Then 43 miles continue on the Willamette with swift flow

to Corvallis, where the current slows for another 82 miles to Newberg. From there the gradient flattens further while shoreline development and motorboats multiply through a languid 22 miles to the mandatory left-shore takeout at West Linn, above Willamette Falls, which lacks both passage and portage possibilities. The low dam, oddly arced across the river at the brink of the falls, is the only impoundment on the entire main-stem Willamette. In all, 189 miles can be paddled with relative ease.

The Oregon Parks Department, Willamette Riverkeeper, and local partners maintain a water trail along much of the Willamette's length with occasional marked campsites. Other state and municipal parks green the shores, which include gravel

bars or enclaves for camping, and trails through riparian forests at Corvallis, Salem, Willamette Mission State Park, the mouth of the Molalla River, and more. Islands and remote sandbars offer additional secluded spots for eddying out. Dozens of access areas and roads on both sides make shuttles easy for trips of any length.

Just below this run, and dammed at its brink, Willamette Falls' forty-one-foot drop is the largest waterfall in volume of flow throughout the West and second-largest in the nation, after Niagara. Even though it's located in the urban fringe of Portland, the falls is mostly invisible from roads; the remarkable sight can be clearly seen only by boating up the Willamette from downstream accesses. Pacific tides cycle up the Columbia and lower Willamette Rivers to the falls.

Willamette habitat is acutely reduced from past grandeur, but it is still impressive. The river was the target of dramatic cleanup efforts in the 1970s that eliminated most sewage and industrial effluent. A greenway proposal to link riverfront parks with continuous public open space was courageously promoted by Governors Tom McCall and Robert Straub in the 1970s but fell victim to farmer and political resistance in following years. Now efforts are underway to reinstate some of the river's complexity in sloughs and back channels that have been reduced through two centuries of systematic farming, channelization, levees, and riprap, and to reclaim some of the river's ability to spread out during floods and thereby diminish high-water damage downstream, recharge groundwater, and reinstate habitat.

One might think this kind of easy trip on a free-flowing river through settled country would be common, but it's not. California's Sacramento River has similar qualities, with big year-round flows for 154 miles from Redding to Colusa, but industrial agriculture there is more intrusive. The Willamette offers uniquely carefree canoeing through a cultural as well as natural landscape.

Although a riparian corridor several miles wide with multiple sloughs and islands has been reduced to a single channel in many places, the immediate frontage of the Willamette is still mostly forested. This mix of cottonwoods and Douglas firs thrives near the mouth of the Molalla River.

DESCHUTES RIVER | Oregon

LENGTH: 6 to 98 miles

WHITEWATER: Class 2-4; portage at Sherars Falls by vehicle

SEASON: summer, fall

GAUGE: Madras

PERMIT: yes

CAMPING: yes

OUTFITTERS: guided trips, raft and kayak rentals

HIGHLIGHTS: big summertime whitewater, canyons, long desert trip, fishing

The Deschutes begins with snowmelt and groundwater, drops into desert terrain, and then aims northward in the rain shadow of the Cascade Mountains. Here the river cuts through the Mutton Mountains south of Maupin.

FOLLOWING SPREAD: Two popular boating sections of the 98-mile-long lower Deschutes are separated by the unrunnable Sherars Falls, where American Indians still dipnet for salmon. Through-boaters require vehicle portage for several miles circumventing the falls (left). The Deschutes carves against basalt walls that rise vertically from the lower river (right).

Runoff from the eastern slope of the Cascade Mountains drops to the Deschutes—world renowned among trout anglers, hot spot for whitewater rafting, and lifeline of desert canyons linking glaciated mountains to the Columbia River. Permits are required, but are usually not difficult to get.

From Highway 26, north of Madras, 98 miles of runoff push northward with big-volume Class 2–3+ rapids. First, 20 miles of glassy water and riffles penetrate golden and blackened basalt canyons to Trout Creek access. Then the rapids pick up powerfully through flooded rock gardens. Ample water all summer is due to voids in the basin's hardened lava that retain groundwater; the Cascade Mountains' snowmelt lingering in summer; and Warm Springs Dam, upstream, which compensates for desiccating irrigation diversions farther up.

Below Highway 26, landing on the left shore is off-limits through the Warm Springs Reservation for 29 miles except with a permit from the tribes. Stay on the east side for BLM campsites. At 14 miles below Trout Creek, the river cuts an enchanting path through the Mutton Mountains. Multiple Deschutes access areas make one-day, overnight, or longer trips possible.

The river bisects Maupin—bustling on summer weekends with day-trip floaters above and below. Everyone must exit 6 miles downriver at Sandy Beach. Just below, unrunnable Sherars Falls separates the 52-mile upper canyon from 42 miles below.

Reenter after shuttling 2 miles by vehicle, or start the lower reach at Buck Hollow ramp for several days of whitewater, basalt cliffs, and campsites. Afternoon winds can be formidable, and

motorboats might mar the quiet, but this reach offers some of the best river travel in the drylands of the interior Northwest. Take out above Interstate 84 east of The Dalles.

Far to the south, the upper Deschutes also offers a suite of paddling possibilities on gentle water interspersed with waterfalls and rapids toothed by jagged lava. The town of Bend has developed one of the West's model urban greenways along the Deschutes with foot and bike trails, a constructed whitewater course where a hazardous dam was removed, and urban amenities only a block from the river.

The lower Deschutes tours a wonderland of deep basalt canyons glowing gold in evening light. This tranquil interlude from whitewater appears at Trestle Hole Island below Sherars Falls.

JOHN DAY RIVER | Oregon

LENGTH: 44 to 225 miles, including the North Fork

WHITEWATER: Class 1-2; one Class 3+; several Class 3 rapids on the North Fork

SEASON: spring, early summer for rafts, into July for canoes and kayaks

GAUGE: Service Creek (main stem), Monument (North Fork)

PERMIT: yes, below Spray on the main stem, and limited

CAMPING: yes

OUTFITTERS: guided trips, raft and kayak rentals

HIGHLIGHTS: long semiwild trip, savanna and dryland canyons, campsites, fishing

The North Fork of the John Day flows from fir and pine forests of the Blue Mountains and then through pine and grass savanna.

For an easy canoe, kayak, or raft trip winding for days or even weeks through remote dryland country, this river has few equals, and none in the Pacific coastal states. The main stem offers 117 miles of boating through canyons and ranchlands, with additional miles both above and below the popular Service Creek to Cottonwood reach. The North Fork can be added for a trip beginning in coniferous forest and transitioning through pine savanna to semiarid canyons and prairie-steppe grasslands—all told, a remarkable geographic tour of the interior Northwest.

Beauty and wildness here are a bit subtle if compared to the greatest wild rivers of the West, but the John Day offers compelling charms. The main stem presents one Class 3–4 drop, but otherwise the whitewater is unthreatening to experienced canoeists, intermediate kayakers, and beginning rafters.

Campsites are plentiful. Permits, available online from the BLM, are not difficult to get except for busy weekends (Memorial Day is extreme), and the weather is usually good, especially for the latter half of the April to May rafting season, stretched into July of most years for canoes and kayaks. All this makes the John Day the choice for anyone seeking a relatively carefree multiday semiwilderness trip.

Many boaters subdivide the main stem into two sections. A 48-mile reach runs from Service Creek (Highway 207 bridge) to Clarno (Highway 218 bridge), and a swifter, wilder, lower 69 miles continues from the Clarno Highway 218 bridge to Cottonwood access at Highway 206. Four miles below Clarno, a turbulent rapid usually requires a long left-side portage of canoes; rafts splash through. Then many miles tour a wonderland of

golden basalt canyons with vertical walls rising hundreds of feet and grassland-steppe ridgelines that invite walkers to sweeping panoramas. The main stem is famous for smallmouth bass fishing in summer, and it's helpful to rid this native salmon and steelhead stream of those exotic predators.

As a separate trip or an add-on that makes the John Day one of the longest river journeys in the West, the North Fork flows swiftly from Highway 395 south of Ukiah to the main stem, with mostly Class 2 rapids, though several reach Class 3 or 3+ at flows above 2,500 cfs. For those not continuing down the main stem, take out in 44 miles at Monument or in another 17 miles at Kimberly and the main-stem confluence.

From Kimberly, well-supplied boaters can con-tinue down the main stem for 23 miles to Service Creek, then onward for a week to Cottonwood and even another 20 miles to the John Day's lowest takeout at McDonald access (watch for it—no bridge!). From Highway 395 on the North Fork to McDonald, the John Day expedition totals 225 miles—nearly the length of the Grand Canyon—with spectacular scenery and only one major rapid.

The main-stem John Day includes two back-to-back reaches of 48 and 69 miles with excellent canoeing water and only one major rapid. Basalt cliffs tower hundreds of feet above this river of desert canyons and dryland steppes.

GRANDE RONDE RIVER | Oregon

LENGTH: 40 to 91 miles

WHITEWATER: Class 2-3

SEASON: late spring, summer

GAUGE: Troy

PERMIT: yes, at put-in, no limit

CAMPING: yes

OUTFITTERS: guided trips, raft and kayak rentals

HIGHLIGHTS: multiday Class 2 trip, spring and summer run for families

For an outing of three days to a week, with mild whitewater, surrounded by beauty that's more gracefully welcoming than harshly rugged, and running with adequate flows for most of summer, the Grande Ronde in northeastern Oregon is ideal.

This sweet summertime float begins on the Wallowa River at the Highway 82 crossing (Minam Store, with hotel, shuttles, and full service for boaters), runs 10 miles down that swift tributary with a few sizable waves and holes, merges into the Grande Ronde, then continues for another 31 miles to Mud Creek access or another 6 miles to Troy.

This whole trip is an idyll of ponderosa pine forest, grassland savanna, bold basalt outcrops, cliffs that step up as hardened lava flows, and swift but unthreatening water for beginning rafters, intermediate kayakers, and seasoned canoeists. Campsites call out from grassy benches beneath the pines, and ridgelines entice walkers to overlooks.

Most floaters take out at Mud Creek, but more awaits beyond. For 19 miles below Troy, Class 2 waters funnel into wave trains past ranchland and mountains decked out in pines and grass. At Boggan's Oasis restaurant and the Highway 129 bridge, take out, break for a milkshake, or continue for 32 more wild miles through the Grande Ronde's increasingly arid lower canyon. Just a few miles up from the Snake River, The Narrows presents a two-part vortex of Class 3 whitewater, reaching Class 4- in springtime, followed shortly by Bridge Rapid. Take out at Heller Bar ramp on the Snake River south of Clarkston, Washington.

The Grande Ronde is an easier alternative to rivers such as the Rogue, where Class 3–4 whitewater is more demanding, permits are required

The Grande Ronde River flows with mostly easy rafting for nearly 100 miles to the Snake River. Basalt cliffs and ponderosa pines rise above the lower river downstream from the Highway 129 bridge in Washington.

in advance, and crowds flock in summer. Early June and holiday weekends at the Grande Ronde are busy, but quiet awaits at most other times. This stream is the perfect, relatively easy summer escape until levels in dry years might drop too low in August.

Though mostly Class 1 and 2, the Grande Ronde concludes with three larger rapids in quick succession as the stream nears its confluence with the Snake River.

OWYHEE RIVER | Oregon

LENGTH: 67 miles, with another 36 miles upstream

WHITEWATER: Class 3-4; upper run, Class 4 with one Class 5+ portage

SEASON: March to June with ample snowmelt; April and May of a normal year; no boating on dry years

GAUGE: Rome

PERMIT: yes, self register at put-in, no limits

CAMPING: yes

OUTFITTERS: guided trips

HIGHLIGHTS: intricate desert rock formations, canyons, whitewater

At Lower Greeley Camp, the Owyhee canyon walls catch the luminous warm tones of a desert sunset.

The Owyhee canyons are among the most rugged and remote in the West, and the river carving them offers a stellar whitewater cruise during a fickle, short springtime. Unlike the elegant sandstone canyons of the Colorado Plateau, these are more jagged and made of somber, hot, dark, volcanic basalt, often rising in spectacular columns and pinnacles.

Rafters and kayakers enjoy the splendor of cliffs towering a thousand feet, bizarre geologic formations from molten sources, lively rapids, and inviting campsites. Hikes to the rim or rock outcrops overlook the river's narrow slot in a vast desert. Beware of rattlesnakes. Pictographs and historic ranch remains round out this tour of a western enclave that few people otherwise see.

The most popular run is a 50-mile tour from Rome—where Highway 95 crosses on the river's only bridge—to the BLM's Birch Creek access via dirt road. Some boaters continue another 12 miles to Leslie Gulch with its gravel road and museum of geologic wonders, though most of the added river mileage is flatwater behind Owyhee Dam.

Dependent on erratic snowfall in Nevada and southern Idaho mountains, runoff in the 1,000 to 4,000 cfs range is suited for rafting. Swift water is spiced with Class 3 and a few Class 4 drops. Low-water trips are possible down to 400 cfs with inflatable kayaks, though sharp rocks become consequential hazards. On drought years flows never reach boatable level; on others they continue for several weeks to two months. Volatile weather can bring snow and freezing temperatures anytime in April or so—prepare for anything! In spite of these limitations, the Owyhee trip is one of the most exceptional in the deserts of the West.

Above the Highway 95 bridge at Rome, another 36-mile section offers an intensified Owyhee. The steep put-in road to Three Forks becomes impassably greasy when wet. Long reaches of flatwater are punctuated with rapids, and boaters encounter the Class 5+ Widowmaker and its arduous lining or portage—altogether a run for experts or professionally outfitted trips. Farther upriver, wilderness sojourns can be undertaken with kayaks or canoes on several low-volume tributaries with occasional portages.

OPPOSITE: The lower Owyhee, from Rome to Birch Creek or onward to Owyhee Reservoir at Leslie Gulch, challenges boaters with Class 3 and Class 4 whitewater. Here the river rushes through Montgomery Rapid in the narrow canyon.

Iron Point looms 800 feet above the Owyhee.

WHITE SALMON RIVER | Washington

LENGTH: 12 miles, usually done as day trips of 7 and 5 miles

WHITEWATER: Class 3-4, plus two drops that are often portaged

SEASON: spring, summer, fall; all year for savvy paddlers

GAUGE: Underwood; 300 to 1,500 cfs

PERMIT: no

CAMPING: no

OUTFITTERS: guided trips

HIGHLIGHTS: whitewater, dramatic portages, rain forest gorge

The enchanted gorge of the White Salmon tumbles with frigid, volcanic springflows from the flanks of celestial Mount Adams to the Columbia River. Packed with excitement and beauty deep within mossy clefts of an intensely green fantasyland, these runs are for the advanced boater or for fit paddlers with a capable guide.

From BZ Corner to Buck Creek (Northwestern Lakes Road), 7 miles of snowmelt and springflows careen with powerful Class 3–4 rapids and twelve-foot Husum Falls, often portaged.

Below is the "lower-lower" White Salmon, tamer but still relentless with Class 3+ paddling. In the midst of one drop just above Steelhead Falls, boaters stop abruptly for an adventurous left-side portage and wade on a flooded basalt shelf by clutching an anchored guy rope with one hand while wrestling boats with the other hand at the wave-battered ledge. Surprise log blockages can be a problem—a reason to go with local paddlers or consult with them. American Whitewater's website posts hazard notifications when it gets them.

One waterfall on each of the lower White Salmon's rafting runs is lined or portaged by most boaters. Steelhead Falls lies just upstream from the photo.

OPPOSITE: Kayaker David Hanson relaxes momentarily between drops of the lower White Salmon. The removal of Condit Dam in 2011 opened the lower river and its enchanting rain forest gorge to paddling here, and it removed a barrier that had blocked salmon migration for decades.

Just an hour from Portland, Oregon, the shuttle along this canyon-bound, paved road couldn't be easier, and ample water runs all year—unusual for such a small river. Drysuited boaters love this reach in winter, as the groundwater continues to flow and the climate is moderated from the interior's bitter chill by Pacific winds and soaking storms that parade up the Columbia Gorge from the ocean.

This river was saved from hydropower threats in the 1970s when local guardians rallied to defeat plans for seven dams, leading eventually to National Wild and Scenic River designation. Then in 2011, the 125-foot-high Condit Dam was blasted away, freeing the lowest 5 miles. This largest dam removal in the United States up to that time made possible today's "lower-lower" run. The bathtub ring of the former reservoir remains subtly evident, but it has rapidly greened with moss and new growth. Symbolic of dam-removal possibilities elsewhere, the canyon's recovery is seen at the former Condit Dam location, 3 miles above the Columbia in a tight slot just below tributary waterfalls that spray directly into the river.

Additional outstanding and challenging Class 3–5 whitewater runs in Washington's Cascade Mountains include sections of the Middle Fork Snoqualmie, Skykomish, North Fork Skykomish, and Wenatchee Rivers.

Rapids of the White Salmon River
pitch downward beneath the bridge
at BZ Corner.

YAKIMA RIVER | Washington

PACIFIC NORTHWEST

LENGTH: 17 miles, with intermediate access

WHITEWATER: Class 1+

SEASON: spring, summer, fall

GAUGE: Umtanum

PERMIT: no

CAMPING: yes

OUTFITTERS: rental rafts and kayaks

HIGHLIGHTS: gentle flows, Class 1 dryland canyon, easy access

In the Pacific Northwest, the rain-soaked, snow-covered western slope of the Cascade Mountains excels in rivers bursting with life, but the dry eastern side has complementary attractions. The Yakima River of central Washington channels snowmelt past Ellensburg and then through a semiarid canyon that has few equals for both ease of paddling and simple logistics. A paved road alongside offers ready access to summerlong flows, ideal for shuttles, including bicycles.

Clear water ripples through bend after bend while mountains ramp skyward, some in sheer basalt cliffs and some with grassy slopes above statuesque ponderosa pines rooted on floodplains. Fremont cottonwoods shade the flats while red osier dogwoods tint waterfronts maroon. Overnighters can eddy out at BLM tracts or commercial facilities. Anglers cast for introduced and native trout, fishing from driftboats and banks.

The Yakima River Canyon Scenic Byway (Route 821) winds the canyon's length. At the upper end, a few miles south of Ellensburg, Ringer access is reached from a short spur west of the highway. Nine miles lead to Umtanum Campground with access at a footbridge. Eight more riffling miles end at Roza Recreation Site and backwaters of a dam that lacks a portage route.

With gentle riffles throughout, this scenic canyon is a river trip for almost any paddler.

The Yakima River offers an easily reached, summerlong, and gently riffling passage through volcanic canyonlands downstream from Ellensburg.

280   AMERICA'S GREAT RIVER JOURNEYS

While morning mist evaporates, cottonwoods and red osier dogwoods line the shores of the Yakima upstream of the Umtanum Creek Recreation Area.

SKAGIT RIVER | Washington

PACIFIC NORTHWEST

LENGTH: 10 to 105 miles

WHITEWATER: Class 1-2; upper run with Class 3

SEASON: summer, fall

GAUGE: Marblemount, Concrete

PERMIT: no

CAMPING: yes

OUTFITTERS: guided trips on the upper river

HIGHLIGHTS: large northwestern river, salmon, river tour from mountains to salt water

As the principal river of Washington's North Cascade Mountains, the Skagit churns in whitewater at upper reaches, swells with runoff from salmon-spawning tributaries, and pushes out to Puget Sound as one of the longest free-flowing lengths of river emptying into the Pacific. Few streams on the West Coast offer the chance to boat from rugged mountains to salt water, which is relatively easy to do here.

Seattle City Light dams block headwaters, but then the maturing Skagit downstream from Newhalem flushes with forceful Class 2–3 rapids for 9 miles to Copper Creek. From there to La Conner, in Puget Sound, the Skagit runs 95 miles with strong currents but no major rapids or dams. Extreme high and low levels can present log hazards.

From Copper Creek to Rockport access, 20 miles flow with swift blue water through Cascade Mountain forests. Just below Rockport, the Sauk River—with several whitewater reaches of its own—joins from the south, delivering silty runoff sourced at the towering icy mass of Glacier Peak, the only Cascade stratovolcano so remote that it's not visible from a road.

This middle Skagit has the look of an Alaskan river with broad, chilled waters washing across immense gravel bars, cottonwoods thick along shorelines, and pink salmon returning in autumn by the hundreds of thousands.

Eight miles below the Sauk confluence, a brief window on a northbound straightaway opens with a view to the heavenly Mount Baker and its deeply crevassed glaciers. Catching a clear day for this scene is a rare treat given the rainy, snowy weather of the North Cascades, but if the sky is clear, this is an extraordinary river-to-mountain view.

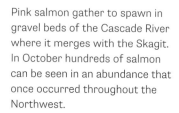

Pink salmon gather to spawn in gravel beds of the Cascade River where it merges with the Skagit. In October hundreds of salmon can be seen in an abundance that once occurred throughout the Northwest.

OPPOSITE: With the longest dam-free canoe trip in Washington, the Skagit River pushes through its final sizable rapid downstream of Newhalem. Strong clear flows—tinted blue green by distant headwater glaciers—continue for 100 miles to Puget Sound.

The power of this big stream pushes relentlessly but smoothly to a boat ramp above Sedro-Woolley. Levees then diminish the nature of the waterway, but it curves onward for 25 miles into tidal zones downstream from Mount Vernon. An unusual "distributary," the river splits at an island with an immense logjam accreted to its upstream face. Staying right, boaters can continue into the salt water of Puget Sound and, with careful navigation staying right of Hawk Point, angle northward among sloughs to a long rock jetty. A gap near the jetty's eastern end leads to the Swinomish Channel's northbound approach to the picturesque and festive seaport La Conner, with takeout docks.

Though traversed by few boaters, the Skagit's mountains-to-saltwater odyssey offers a unique opportunity to travel on a river from upper reaches to sea, all in a journey of four days.

While Seattle City Light's dams diminish the Skagit's once legendary runs of salmon, this basin remains the healthiest anadromous fishery in Puget Sound and one of the best in the United States south of Alaska. Further damming, proposed at Copper Creek and on the Sauk River, was averted, and a nuclear power plant proposed in the 1970s for the lower river was stopped. The Skagit and its Sauk, Suiattle, and Cascade tributaries were added to the National Wild and Scenic Rivers System in 1978. Taken together, these represent one of the most complete networks of natural rivers protected in the Wild and Scenic program.

The Skagit's robust flow of glacially silted blue water, gravel bars, direct passage from high mountains to sea, and surviving runs of salmon make this relatively easy and accessible journey a special river experience.

OPPOSITE: The majestic rise of Mount Baker fills the background in a view that opens only briefly from the Skagit River 8 miles downstream from the Sauk River confluence. Clouds normally obscure the iconic peak.

A canoe voyage down the Skagit ends in salt water at picturesque La Conner, reached in the estuary of Swinomish Channel. Mount Baker graces the background.

ALASKA

Alaska ranks as the preeminent wild river region of the United States and the world. Hundreds of rivers penetrate unspoiled landscapes. Here one-third of America's fresh water flows across one-fifth of the nation's landscape. The tenth-largest river in this state is still larger than the Colorado in the Grand Canyon.

Runnable rivers are too many to count, but unquestionably classic are the Tatshenshini-Alsek combination, the Copper with its massive volume tearing at the edges of glaciers, and any number of Brooks Range rivers, such as the Noatak and Sheenjek.

The rewards of Alaskan rivers are great with astonishing beauty, wildness like few places on earth, vast distances of untouched terrain, and wildlife in herds, packs, flocks, and schools that exist elsewhere only in legends.

But getting there is difficult. It's not just a multiday drive to reach Alaska, but a two-day flight from many parts of the country. Then, most river-trip access is by chartered bush planes to remote gravel bars or lakes. Guide services are expensive, and so is outfitting your own trip. Humbling to all, grizzly bears reign undeniably at the top of the food chain. The weather can be brutal, the bugs maddening. The season is short, and consequences of foul weather, equipment failure, or injuries can be severe. But with proper precautions, the challenges are all worth it to experience the wildest rivers in America.

TATSHENSHINI AND ALSEK RIVERS | Alaska

LENGTH: 130 miles

WHITEWATER: Class 3, big volume; Class 4 when high

SEASON: June to mid-September

GAUGE: Dry Bay (Glacier Bay National Park and Preserve)

PERMIT: yes, and tightly limited

CAMPING: yes

OUTFITTERS: guided trips, rental rafts

HIGHLIGHTS: glaciers, wildlife, large river, wilderness

PREVIOUS SPREAD: Mount Fairweather glows at sunset above Alaska's Alsek River.

The Alsek River collects frigid runoff from the largest nonpolar ice fields in the world and pulses through the skyscraping Coast Range to the Gulf of Alaska.

FOLLOWING SPREAD: Near the end of the Tatshenshini expedition, Alsek Lake appears as a bulge of flatwater behind an island that splits the Alsek River's massive flow into left- and right-side channels. Icebergs calve into the water from the face of glaciers grinding down from 15,325-foot Mount Fairweather.

In a class by itself, the Tatshenshini and Alsek River raft trip has no match for a massive river through mountains of ice age grandeur with glaciers, wilderness, whitewater, and wildlife. Many travelers consider this journey the most spectacular wilderness river trip on the continent. As the International Union for Conservation of Nature stated, "The Tatshenshini-Alsek river system . . . is one of the world's most beautiful and magnificent."

The trip starts on the growing Tatshenshini in Yukon Territory, cuts through the northwestern corner of British Columbia, and in 100 miles merges with the Alsek for a river of truly gigantic size. This river crosses into Alaska and ends near sea level in Dry Bay of Glacier Bay National Park and Preserve.

Whitewater on the first day of the seven- to ten-day expedition challenges boaters with turbulence capable of throwing passengers out or possibly even flipping rafts. After an 8-mile canyon, the rapids ease. However, the volume and speeding current at 10 miles per hour make eddy lines hazardous to smaller boats. Consuming holes seem to appear at random, and the sheer size of the river and distance to shore in icy water pose hazards even without abrupt drops.

With no intermediate access or evacuation route by road, the river passes through multiple fault-block terranes and doubles in volume again and again. In the grand scale of the place, tributaries that would be recognized as major rivers elsewhere go unnoticed. Peaks rise thousands of feet, mostly inaccessible behind moats and slopes of tangled, bearish brush or rocky debris; however a compelling all-day hike reaches lofty meadows immediately north of the Sediments Creek campsite, about 50 miles below the put-in.

As boaters enter the snow-covered Coast Range in the lower third of the route, glaciers appear in the mountains' cirque basins, then multiply in length and breadth from the world's largest nonpolar ice cap. A dozen or more glaciers can be seen at once, their paths encroaching lower and lower and then onto the valley floor. Wildlife includes one of the continent's highest concentrations of brown (grizzly) bears, Dall sheep, bald eagles, moose, and wolves.

At Walker Glacier, travelers can stroll just a few steps from camp onto the ice and wander up to yawning crevasses that open to depthless blue and black voids within the ice. Near the trip's end, at Alsek Lake, icebergs the size of battleships break from glaciers and calve into the water, their plunge producing minor tidal waves; don't camp at the waterline! Behind this kinetic foreground, Mount Fairweather rears up 15,325 feet—vertical relief directly from sea to summit unequaled worldwide.

River travel here is not without challenges. Permits from Glacier Bay National Park and Preserve in the United States are in great demand, with a waiting list of two or three years. The launch in Canada requires a passport. The takeout involves a chartered bush-plane flight back to Yakutat, or more likely Haines—a good urban base with access to rental gear for those who have flown or taken the ferryboat north from the "outside." Whitewater hazards on the first day are real, and anyone who gets a weeklong trip without several bone-chilling, hat-clutching, horizontal rainstorms is fortunate.

Walker Glacier extends from stormy heights of Mount Fairweather and almost to the edge of the Alsek River, allowing travelers to stroll onto its icy surface and tempting ridgelines.

The flow is enormous—often 100,000 cfs on the lower Alsek. This compares to a typical 8,000 cfs for the Grand Canyon of the Colorado, noted for big water. But unlike that canyon, the Alsek's width reaches 2 miles in places. Exposure is edgy, and safer with the security of two or more rafts per trip. Take all precautions regarding bears.

Not the least of challenges, passage through Alsek Lake—the preferred route for scenery and campsites near the end of the trip—may be complicated by ice jams within the lake. When these materialize through the combined vagaries of calving, wind, and currents, they require a must-do row above the lake's inlet across monolithic

currents to the right side of the river to avoid being swept irrevocably through the river-left inlet to the lake and onward against the ice. This ominous possibility must be scouted from the left shore well above the lake's inlet, requiring careful map work and stopping at least a full mile upstream from the inlet.

While experienced teams of independent boaters can manage the Tatshenshini-Alsek adventure, a commercial outfitter is likely the preferred way for many people to see this remarkable landscape.

The Tatshenshini became the river conservation battle of the decade in the 1990s when a sprawling copper mine was proposed—similar to outsized mountaintop removals in West Virginia—to decapitate two lofty peaks between the Tatshenshini and Alsek Rivers. Tailings ponds of permanently acidic wastewater, intended for storage indefinitely, would have been perched at the continent's most active fault zone—seismically active annually if not daily—imperiling one of the world's greatest salmon fisheries. Haul roads would have been knifed into hundreds of miles of virgin country. Political battles culminated in 1993 with British Columbia's designation of Tatshenshini-Alsek Provincial Park. These river corridors, with adjacent parklands all totaling 21 million acres, are now the world's largest protected landscape.

Conservationists in Canada and the United States won the battle against the Windy Craggy copper mine in the mountains above the Tatshenshini and Alsek Rivers. Designation of a provincial preserve linked other protected areas of Alaska, Yukon, and British Columbia into the largest parkland complex worldwide. Here Mount Fairweather pierces an uncommonly blue sky above the lower Alsek.

COPPER RIVER | Alaska

LENGTH: 52 to 265 miles

WHITEWATER: Class 2, but extremely high volume

SEASON: June to August

GAUGE: Cordova

PERMIT: no

CAMPING: yes

OUTFITTERS: guided trips, rental rafts for the lower Copper

HIGHLIGHTS: enormous river, long wilderness trip, glaciers, wildlife

Ten miles below the Slana put-in, the Copper River is already wide, with braided channels, gravel bars sprouting willows, black spruces bristling from shore, and rainstorms billowing over Mount Sanford—16,237 feet high but obscured in clouds.

With easier access and less-challenging white-water than the famed Tatshenshini-Alsek trip, and without permit requirements, the Copper River of southcentral Alaska is a world-class wilderness destination in its own right. Here one can raft for a week or two on glacial runoff that swells to staggering amounts—even higher volumes than the Alsek—through wild terrain with brown bears, eagles, and wolves; alongside glacial walls 300 feet tall; beneath peaks that climb to 16,000 feet in the distance; and past incongruous, drifting sand dunes fit for the Mojave but rising directly from this northern river for 12 miles.

Flowing from the Wrangell and Chugach Mountains, this is one of only three megarivers that transect Alaska's supremely mountainous southcentral Coast Range. The phenomenon of big water beneath skyscraping peaks thrills in its scale and scope.

Multiple access points make raft trips in the 40- to 70-mile range possible. Better, a major expedition beckons from an upper put-in on the Slana River at the Nabesna Road bridge, just south of Highway 1 east of Chistochina. A half mile of shallow water feeds the widening Copper. From there it's 265 miles to the mouth at Flag Point Bridge and the head of the Copper River Delta, where taking out requires vehicle shuttle (bus service by arrangement) for 26 miles to Cordova. This coastal burg lacks road access to the Alaska highway system, so travelers schlep their gear from bus to ferryboat for five hours of open-sea transit to Valdez, where Highway 4 leads north to reconnect with the continental road system.

Relentless currents whisk rafts 10 miles per hour. Campsites appear as vast gravel bars or on grassy banks where one might imagine a

At a Copper River gravel bar by the mouth of the Nadina River, rafters Greg and Mary Bettencourt and Ann Vileisis relax before preparing dinner under the essential shelter of a rain tarp.

OPPOSITE: Ann Vileisis rows steadily as Childs Glacier encroaches directly on the Copper River's current for 2 miles. Calving icebergs can create waves that can be troublesome to boaters.

climatically severe version of the silty, braided, and cottonwood-lined shores of the Missouri or Sacramento Rivers in the year 1750 before those arteries were touched by settlement, farms, levees, and dams.

Along the way, a dozen tributaries disgorge 5,000 to 20,000 cfs each, and then the Chitina River doubles the Copper's size. In some places the oceanic stream spans 3 miles, pushing indomitably downward like a lake that is tilted from one end to the other.

Interior Alaska's drier climate recedes as the river penetrates the heart of the coastal mountains and brushes against the continent's largest ice masses sourced on some of North America's highest mountains in the Saint Elias Range to the east, and also from forbidding peaks of the Chugach Mountains to the west. The farther downriver one

travels, the more rainfall increases. Temperatures plummet, travelers zip up their rain gear, and ice and snow crowd nearer as glaciers approach river level. Miles Glacier nearly touches the Copper from the east. When camping there, one hears thunderous booms and cracks of the ice's inevitable advance.

Then, for a mile on the west side, a 200-foot-tall front of Childs Glacier pushes directly into the river. Swift currents undermine the terminal ice and can trigger skyscraper icebergs to collapse into the water. Here boaters stay in midstream—away from the disintegrating glacial front and also away from the opposite shore, where tidal waves created by collapsing ice can crest and break like a tsunami as they enter shallows near the river's shore.

As on the Tatshenshini, rafts are the essential craft given the forceful flows, frigid water, powerful eddy lines, high winds, rainy weather, and long distances. Ample drinking water should be carried, and for long trips, resupply must be sought at small clear-water tributaries. Mosquitoes hover thick at some campsites, and bears require full precautions in food storage and when hiking.

Above Miles Glacier, Abercrombie Rapid is a series of rolling or breaking waves, normally run without complications at a safe distance from shoreline boulders. But owing to exposure, it warrants caution; any upset would be in swift icy water with little chance to reach shore. It's possible to do this as a one-boat trip, but I do not recommend that, as storm-induced flows can top 200,000 cfs, and to reach the shore from the center of the river I've needed twenty minutes of rowing at full speed directly toward the bank.

River aficionados on the Copper can marvel at the transparency of ongoing geologic and hydrologic processes that are only subtly evident on older and tamer rivers. Massive amounts of silt cause sand and gravel bars to form and reform constantly. Shorelines erode and islands are built

up and torn down. Suspended silt is so thick that it hisses and scratches audibly against the bottom of the boat. Floating ice in spring gouges new pathways. Whirlpools spin where submerged boulders remain unseen. Seals migrate 40 miles up from salt water to feed on salmon. Though hidden in turbid currents, those fish swim upstream by the hundreds of thousands and fall prey to bears wading in the river. Summertime twilight lingers for hours as the northern sun drops not directly toward the horizon but at an acute angle northward and disappears only in the middle of the night.

The scenery is not as spectacular and the trip not as wild as the Tatshenshini-Alsek, but the Copper is packed with adventure and extremes of water, mountains, weather, glaciers, and wildness found only in Alaska.

An aerial view from 35,000 feet above the Copper River Delta shows a Pleistocene universe of ice fields, glaciers, and pioneering forests sprouting on thawed flats and mountainsides. In the center of this scene, the river pools in Miles Lake. Miles Glacier encroaches from the right while Childs Glacier advances from the left.

SHEENJEK RIVER | Alaska

LENGTH: 288 miles (shorter trips possible)

WHITEWATER: Class 1-2

SEASON: June to September

GAUGE: none; inquire at the Arctic National Wildlife Refuge in Fairbanks

PERMIT: no

CAMPING: yes

OUTFITTERS: possible guided trips

HIGHLIGHTS: long wilderness Brooks Range trip

Seen from a rocky perch upstream from Double Mountain, braided channels gather as the Sheenjek River takes form beneath the Romanzof Mountains—the highest subrange of Alaska's Brooks Range.

Here at the far reaches of America are the rivers of Alaska's Brooks Range, which are among the wildest waterways in the world. From the heights of starkly beautiful mountains, dozens of streams carry snowmelt north to the Arctic Ocean or south to the Yukon River. Some meander hundreds of miles through untouched country. Among the longest, the Sheenjek begins in northeast Alaska within the Romanzof Mountains—the highest apex of the greater Brooks Range—and winds 250 miles to the Porcupine River, which then concludes its final 40 miles to the Yukon.

The Sheenjek presents a rare chance to travel for twenty or thirty days with scarcely a contrail in sight. Like most Alaskan river trips, you need to fly in via bush plane. This is from the native-populated Fort Yukon, reached by small commercial airlines based in Fairbanks. A floatplane can take you to Last Lake or, better, take a fat-tire bush plane another 20 miles, touch down on a gravel bar that your pilot will know about near Double Mountain, and embark on an unforgettable wilderness route back to Fort Yukon.

By the end of July, warm weather has melted most of the aufeis. This is ice that freezes to the bottom of the riverbed in the brittle chill of the Arctic winter. Incoming water freezes on top, eventually accreting to an eight-foot ice cap virtually covering the valley floor upstream from Double Mountain. Even in August some ice may remain and require boaters to carry or drag gear for a few hundred yards.

Tributaries soon augment the flow, and the shoals and ice walls give way to swift currents. Fabulous mountain scenery stands starkly barren with rocky scree and permafrost tundra far north of the Arctic Circle. High ridgelines and summits

A caribou prances across mountaintop tundra above the Sheenjek River.

OPPOSITE: Thick ice persists on the Sheenjek above Double Mountain until late summer. This platform just happened to break up and open the channel in time for the morning's departure.

are wonderfully accessible with rocky scrambles that open views to the braided river and to endless peaks of America's northernmost mountain chain. With some luck, caribou will be seen grazing on lichen. I've found tracks of grizzly bears, wolves, moose, and beavers virtually every time I've stopped on the Sheenjek shores, though I've actually seen little of this wildlife along the river. Native Alaskans have subsisted here for millennia, and wild animals are wary of hunters.

After several days the terrain tapers down to hills and tundra flats, then to boreal forest of spruce, willows, and balsam fir in the vast Yukon Flats National Wildlife Refuge. Frequent Class 2

As the Sheenjek consolidates downstream from Table Mountain, Jon Miller and Lou Brown deftly negotiate Class 2 rapids in their collapsible Ally canoe, well suited for bush-plane access.

OPPOSITE: The Artic sun sets at midnight along the Porcupine River upstream from Fort Yukon.

riffles ease into Class 1 and then flatwater of the lower Sheenjek. Fifty miles above the river's end, a prickly logjam may interrupt the trip with an arduous portage.

Merging into the larger Porcupine, sourced 500 miles to the east, the current continues through bends in seemingly endless wetlands of Yukon Flats. Prepare for bugs! Follow maps closely and, finally, at Homebrew Island—about 2 miles before the Porcupine enters the oceanic Yukon River—detour left into the obscurely small Sucker River slough. Otherwise, the weighty current of the Yukon—America's fifth-largest river—prevents paddling 2 miles upstream to Fort Yukon. After a few miles up the calm waters of the Sucker, a dirt road leads to town. I've missed this cryptic exit, but I managed to walk back to Fort Yukon from near the Sheenjek's mouth and arrange for a motorboat to pick up my gear.

Bugs can be colossally annoying but avoidable on the Sheenjek's breezy gravel bars. Late-season travelers face fewer mosquitoes but chance blustery cold weather in September. Take all precautions regarding grizzly bears. Navigation by map is difficult owing to extreme meandering patterns of the middle and lower Sheenjek.

Given the necessity of bush-plane access to the put-in, this is a trip for portable boats, such as Ally folding canoes, folding kayaks, and inflatable kayaks or canoes, though packing enough gear for a long trip in those craft is a challenge. Small rafts serve well, even with marathons of flatwater.

While the Sheenjek and other Brooks Range rivers lack the tour of glacier landscapes seen on the Tatshenshini, Alsek, and Copper, the wildness of the north is profound and the rivers are striking in their winding paths across a memorable landscape.

EPILOGUE | Safeguarding the Rivers We Love

The first rule when going on a river trip is to keep people safe from the river.

The first rule after the trip is to keep the river safe from people. That, it turns out, is harder to do. Yet the need to prevail is no less important, and the rewards are even greater.

After spending a day or a week floating with the current, immersed in the timeless flow, at home with the ages of rocks, it seems that the river and its life are indomitable, and it's easy to think that our stream will always be there for us. The Grand Canyon, for example, symbolizes permanence. The flow of the Hudson or Klamath, running for tens of thousands of years, might call up feelings of forever to anyone who is open to such thoughts. But good rivers will endure only if people who care about them guard them as if they were their own. The challenge of protecting our rivers is great and—like any day of paddling—it draws on our wits, our skills, and our ability to work together.

This book highlights fifty journeys, and others await for people who want to go further. The possibilities are enlivening, but it's important to note, here at the end of this book, that we've lost far more superb river journeys than we have left to enjoy.

Eighty thousand sizable dams have been built in the United States and affect nearly every major river and most minor ones. Thousands of those dams have eliminated what were once fabulous river trips. Veteran guide Martin Litton recalled that the full 200-mile length of Hells Canyon of the Snake River was once comparable to the Grand Canyon for whitewater and wildness. Half of it, and five of its seven great rapids, are now dammed. The sublime depths of Glen Canyon—upstream from the Grand Canyon—were considered the most beautiful reach of the entire Colorado River, but they're now buried under a reservoir. American Indians thought it impossible that Celilo Falls, of the Columbia, could be silenced. But it was.

The Stanislaus River in California was the most popular whitewater in the West and the deepest limestone canyon on the Pacific coast when it was unnecessarily entombed behind a dam in 1980. Hungry Horse Dam flooded what many considered the best part of the stunning Flathead River system near the border of Glacier National Park. The Tennessee Valley Authority plugged every major tributary in that biologically wondrous river basin, slamming shut the gates of Tellico Dam in 1979 and flooding the Little Tennessee River—a splendid canoeing stream that was also revered by the Cherokee, cherished by Appalachian mountaineers, and home to an endangered fish. On and on the list goes.

Dams are only part of what has diminished the river-running estate of America. Diversions for irrigation and hydropower have depleted and desiccated legendary sections of rivers from the lower Penobscot to the upper Skagit. Levees and channelization have ditched and straightened hundreds of thousands of miles, including the once spectacular cottonwood meanders of the Sacramento and Willamette Rivers as they graced some of the continent's most fruitful wildlife habitat. Farms, cities, suburbia, roads, and railroads have preempted far more riverfronts than they've spared.

In the United States, 6,770 rivers or streams flow for 25 miles or more. These total 417,000 miles. That may seem like a lot, but once the sections blocked by dams are eliminated, along with other incursions, only a small number of rivers have sections suitable for river trips.

Studies by the U.S. Department of the Interior found that only three percent of the river and stream miles of our country retain the "outstandingly remarkable" natural qualities that are prerequisite to a river's

After one of the most intense dam debates in American history, the Stanislaus River in California was unnecessarily buried under 700 feet of flatwater, including this sunrise scene from the base of Mother Rapid, named on Mother's Day, 1967.

enrollment in the National Wild and Scenic Rivers System—a congressionally designated group of prestigious waterways sanctioned by law to remain natural. Started in 1968 with twelve rivers and tributaries, the Wild and Scenic program now includes 290 major rivers, including twenty-seven of the fifty that are featured in this book. This premier river-protection program prohibits dams and other federal projects that would harm the streams. It also encourages local planning efforts to guard shorelines from overdevelopment, and in some cases sets aside limited amounts of open space along the rivers and improves recreation facilities such as access areas. See *Wild and Scenic Rivers: An American Legacy* for full coverage of this important program that helps safeguard many of our finest streams. Other efforts, ranging from the Clean Water Act to local floodplain zoning, can benefit virtually all of America's river mileage.

All fifty rivers covered here have faced threats that would have ruined them if it hadn't been for courageous people who stood up in their rivers' defense during times of need. The featured runs on the Saint John, Allagash, and Penobscot of Maine were slated for damming, as were the Hudson, Delaware, Clarion, Current, Buffalo, Saint Croix, Niobrara, Missouri, Flathead, Salmon, Selway, Snake, Colorado, Tuolumne, Kern, American, Klamath, Rogue, White Salmon, Skagit, and more. The Youghiogheny, Clarion, Potomac, New, Gauley, Rio Grande, Yellowstone, Alsek, Copper, Rogue, and Arkansas have been threatened or damaged by mining. Others have been imperiled by diversions of water to suburbs with booming populations, or by land development, including building houses too close to riverfronts instead of locating investments back from the costly and inevitable hazards of floods.

We continue to face threats to these fifty rivers and to our other remaining natural streams. Even the Grand Canyon of the Colorado—shielded by one of our greatest national parks—faces a triple menace of uranium mine, aerial tram, and megaresort encroachment.

Many organizations are dedicated to protecting our best streams. American Rivers is the nation's principal river conservation group. Based in Washington, DC, it serves as the political connection for people nationwide engaged in saving their streams. American Whitewater and the American Canoe Association work tirelessly on behalf of paddlers and river travelers who realize that they must do what's needed to sustain the rivers they use. Local paddling clubs, from the Canoe Cruisers Association of Greater Washington, DC, to the Willamette Kayak and Canoe Club in Oregon, shoulder this task as well. River Network helps grassroots groups organize and succeed in protection and restoration campaigns. Trout Unlimited and the Native Fish Society strive to see that our wild fish are not driven further toward extinction and that their habitat is sustained. Clean Water Action resists the coal, oil, and gas industries' efforts to roll back the Clean Water Act. Each major river and most minor ones have a homegrown organization dedicated to the life of their stream. Waterkeeper Alliance sponsors many of these as Riverkeeper groups that battle fearlessly for the clarity and health of our water. The National Wildlife Federation, Sierra Club, Wilderness Society, Nature Conservancy, and other organizations also embrace river protection within their broader environmental missions.

Every person who has embarked on any one of these fifty great river journeys—or on other outings—can engage with time, intelligence, and passion to protect and restore a waterway. This is done by joining a conservation group and becoming personally involved with a local or favorite river, wherever it might be.

Learn about your stream. Teach others, especially children and elected officials. Engage politically as an advocate for nature and for the future. Adopt your river as your own.

It takes only one trip, floating downstream in a canoe, kayak, or raft, to know that these rivers are beautiful, essential, and irreplaceable. The rewards that they offer to all of us will be available to the next generation only if we take care of these remarkable places today.

Though some trips down the rivers featured in this book might require only a few hours or a day, an overnight or weeklong journey can take us to places and to times when the rest of the world disappears. We're left with pure and perfect beauty in the flow of nature. Go to these places, be open to these realities, and allow your spirit to soar and your life to be changed, forever, by these rivers.

The Yellowstone River traverses Montana as one of the great rivers of the Rockies and Great Plains, but it faces continuing threats from floodplain development, riprap (rock fill on the banks), oil spills from pipelines and railroads, and construction of a new dam on this nearly dam-free river.

SOURCES

For details about rapids, put-in and takeout locations, and natural history, see selected references to other books, maps, and websites listed here by region. Additional information about permit procedures and more is available at websites maintained by the administering government agencies—the U.S. Forest Service, Bureau of Land Management (BLM), National Park Service, Fish and Wildlife Service, plus some state parks agencies.

For further details about rapids and access, see American Whitewater's website (www.americanwhitewater.org). For flow reports, see U.S. Geological Survey and National Oceanic Atmospheric Administration sites, and for the West, also visit the Dreamflows website (www.dreamflows.com). For instruction, see *River Running: Canoeing, Kayaking, Rowing, Rafting* by Verne Huser and *Canoeing* by the American Red Cross. For longer trips, see *The Wilderness Paddler's Handbook* by Alan Kesselheim.

Statewide guidebooks can be found for all states that have extensive river-running possibilities, and they include details about access, rapids, and logistics. See also websites for shuttle services and outfitters, as well as guides associations, including groups in Oregon, Idaho, and the Colorado River basin.

For a thorough overview of America's rivers and their geography, including narratives about some of the rivers highlighted here, see *America by Rivers*; for photo documentation of rivers nationwide, see *Rivers of America*; and for explanations, photos, and descriptions of the National Wild and Scenic Rivers System—referenced in these fifty river profiles—see *Wild and Scenic Rivers: An American Legacy*—all by Tim Palmer.

The moon rises over the Green River in Desolation Canyon in Utah.

NEW ENGLAND

Allagash Wilderness Waterway, map, National Geographic
The AMC New England Canoeing Guide, Appalachian Mountain Club
Appalachian Whitewater: Volume III, The Northern Mountains, John Connelly and John Porterfield
DeLorme's Map & Guide, Allagash & St. John (out of print, search the internet for a used copy)
Saco River Map and Guide, brochure, Appalachian Mountain Club

APPALACHIAN MOUNTAINS

Appalachian Whitewater: Volume I, The Southern Mountains, Bob Sehlinger et al.
Appalachian Whitewater: Volume II, The Central Mountains, Ed Grove et al.
A Canoeing & Kayaking Guide to West Virginia, Paul Davidson et al.
Canoeing Guide to Western Pennsylvania and Northern West Virginia, Roy Weil and Mary Shaw
Canoeing the Delaware River, Gary Letcher
Chattooga National Wild and Scenic River, map, Chattahoochee National Forest
Clarion River Water Trail, Upper and Middle Sections, Pennsylvania Department of Conservation and Natural Resources
Delaware River Recreation Maps, Delaware River Basin Commission
Keystone Canoeing: A Guide to Canoeable Waters of Eastern Pennsylvania, Edward Gertler
Maryland and Delaware Canoe Trails, Edward Gertler
Pine Creek Water Trail, Map & Guide, Pennsylvania Fish and Boat Commission
The Potomac River: A History & Guide, Garrett Peck
Youghiogheny: Appalachian River, Tim Palmer

DEEP SOUTH

A Canoeing and Kayaking Guide to the Streams of Florida, Volume 1,
Elizabeth F. Carter and John L. Pearce

Suwannee River Wilderness Trail Boat Ramps & Canoe Launches, map,
Suwannee River Management District, www.srwmd.state.
fl.us/documentcenter/home/view/31

MIDWEST

Buffalo National River, map, National Geographic

The Buffalo National River Canoeing Guide, Ozark Society

Buffalo River Handbook, Kenneth L. Smith

Missouri Ozark Waterways, Missouri Conservation Department

Ozark National Scenic Riverways, map, National Park Service

Paddling Northern Wisconsin, Mike Svob

Saint Croix National Scenic Riverway, website with maps,
www.nps.gov/sacn/index.htm

*Whitewater; Quietwater: The Wild Rivers of Wisconsin, Upper
Michigan, & NE Minnesota,* Bob and Jody Palzer

GREAT PLAINS

Cody, Kilgore, and Valentine Quadrangles, maps, U.S. Geological
Survey (nominal mapping of the upper river)

Floating and Recreation on Montana Rivers, Curt Thompson

Niobrara National Scenic River Map, National Park Service,
www.nps.gov/niob/planyourvisit/canoeing-
kayaking-tubing.htm

Paddling Montana, Hank and Carol Fischer

Upper Missouri National Wild and Scenic River, four maps, BLM,
Lewiston, Montana

Yellowstone River Floater's Guide (six maps, Springdale to mouth),
BLM, Billings, Montana

ROCKY MOUNTAINS

Arkansas River Guide, Thomas Rampton

Grand Teton National Park: Snake River Guide, Verne Huser and
Buzz Belknap

*Idaho's Salmon River: A River Runner's Guide to the River of No Return,
Corn Creek to Carey Creek,* Eric J. Newell with Allison J. Newell

Lower Salmon River Boater's Guide, BLM

The Middle Fork of the Salmon: A Wild and Scenic River, map and
guide, U.S. Forest Service

The Middle Fork of the Salmon River, Matt Leidecker

The Salmon: A Wild and Scenic River, map and guide, U.S. Forest
Service

The Snake River: Window to the West, Tim Palmer

The Wild and Scenic Selway River, Bitterroot and Nez Perce
National Forests

The Wild and Scenic Snake River, Hells Canyon National Recreation
Area, U.S. Forest Service

Three Forks of the Flathead River Floating Guide, Flathead
National Forest

Wyoming's Snake River, Verne Huser

SOUTHWEST

Big Bend: Floating the Rio Grande, brochure, National Park Service

Big Bend National Park, maps, Big Bend Natural History Association

Boating in the Monument, National Park Service, www.nps.gov/
dino/planyourvisit/upload/2017DinosaurBoatingInformation-
forwebsite.pdf

Canyonlands River Guide, Bill and Buzz Belknap (Labyrinth-Stillwater
Canyons)

The Colorado River in Grand Canyon: A Guide, Larry Stevens

Desolation River Guide, Loie Belknap Evans and Buzz Belknap

Dinosaur River Guide, Loie Belknap Evans and Buzz Belknap (Flaming
Gorge, Lodore-Whirlpool-Split Mountain Canyons)

The Floater's Guide to Colorado, Doug Wheat

Grand Canyon River Guide, Buzz Belknap

The Lower Canyons of the Rio Grande, Louis F. Aulbach and Joe Butler

River Runners' Guide to Utah and Adjacent Areas, Gary C. Nichols

RiverMaps Guide to the Colorado River in the Grand Canyon, Tom Martin
and Duwain Whitis

San Juan River Guide, Lisa Kearsley

Western Whitewater from the Rockies to the Pacific, Jim Cassady et al.

CALIFORNIA

The American River, Protect American River Canyons

California Whitewater: A Guide to the Rivers, Jim Cassady and
Fryar Calhoun

Field Guide to California Rivers, Tim Palmer

West Coast River Touring: Rogue River Canyon and South, Dick Schwind (out of print, search the internet for a used copy)

PACIFIC NORTHWEST

Deschutes Paddle Trail River Guide, Bend Paddle Trail Alliance (upper river)

Deschutes River Boater's Guide, BLM

Field Guide to Oregon Rivers, Tim Palmer

A Guide to the Rogue River Water Trail, BLM et al. (for upper reaches, Lost Creek Dam to Grants Pass)

A Guide to the Whitewater Rivers of Washington, Jeff Bennett

John Day River Recreation Guide: Kimberly to Tumwater Falls, BLM (main stem)

North Umpqua Wild and Scenic River Users Guide, BLM and U.S. Forest Service

Owyhee, Bruneau, and Jarbidge Wild and Scenic Rivers Boating Guide, BLM

Rogue River Float Guide, BLM

Soggy Sneakers: A Paddler's Guide to Oregon's Rivers, Willamette Kayak and Canoe Club

Wallowa and Grande Ronde Rivers Boating Guide, BLM

Washington Atlas & Gazetteer, DeLorme atlas (map of lower Skagit river and estuary)

The Willamette River Field Guide, Travis Williams and Willamette Riverkeeper

Willamette River Recreation Guide, Oregon State Parks

ALASKA

The Alaska River Guide, Karen Jettmar

Fast & Cold: A Guide to Alaska Whitewater, Andrew Embick

Rafter Dorrie Brownell soaks in the gleam of the Alsek River where glacier-clad peaks whiten the Alaskan backdrop in sublime views, illuminated even as midnight nears in the middle of summer.

ABOUT THE PHOTOGRAPHS

For many years I used a Canon A-1 camera with 17-200 mm FD lenses, but most of the photos here were taken with a Canon 5D digital camera with 17-200 L series zoom lenses and a 50 mm L series lens. For adventures when a small kit is needed, I carry a Fujifilm digital X-E2 with its 18-55 and 55-200 XF zoom lenses. For on-the-water snapshots I use a Canon underwater Powershot.

With the goal of showing rivers and river travel accurately and realistically, I limit myself to minor postphoto adjustments for contrast and color under Apple's very basic iPhoto program. I use no artificial light or filters, and do nothing to alter the content of the photos. The overriding principle of my work is to share with others the beauty and adventures that I've been privileged to see and experience in the natural world and in traveling on our rivers nationwide.

The Middle Fork Coquille River rushes through its woodland corridor in Oregon.

ACKNOWLEDGMENTS

My wife comes first on this list. Ann Vileisis and I met on the Middle Fork of the Salmon River, so what might one expect? Throughout writing this book she has been a perfect companion, valued advisor, sharp editor, tasteful photo critic, gifted author of her own books, and charismatic leader of local conservation efforts along the rivers where we live.

It has been a pleasure to work with Rizzoli associate publisher Jim Muschett, editor Candice Fehrman, and designer Susi Oberhelman.

For the writing and photos, I drew on my own fifty-year history of river running, which intensified once Jim agreed to publish this book. I've done most of my canoeing and rafting as independent trips, sometimes alone, often with Ann, and also with friends. For some of the intense whitewater I went with outfitters for safety, often rowing my own raft. A colorful cast of river aficionados surfaced everywhere I went.

College of the Atlantic (COA) professor Ken Cline jumped at my suggestion to paddle the Saint John. He recruited the extremely capable COA professor Helen Hess and alumnus Bob DeForest, plus six students, for a memorable trip. My paddling buddy from earlier adventures, Travis Hussey, joined me on the Saco. At the Hudson Gorge, a wonderfully personable guide, Marnie Feldman Kohl, took me down the river on her day off from Beaver Brook Outfitters.

At the Delaware, my friend Scott Tilden chauffeured the long drive to the put-in. My Pine Creek experience goes back to forestry professor Peter Fletcher of Penn State University, to whom I shall forever be indebted for first engaging me in river conservation. At the Clarion, Country Squirrel Outfitters were the perfect ticket for logistical help.

Eric Martin of Wilderness Voyageurs on the Youghiogheny has been a helpful friend for years, and before that, Mike McCarty, Jim Prothero, and John Lichter pointed to enlightening paths when I was writing *Youghiogheny: Appalachian River*. I have fond memories of Jim, and thanks to master instructor John for coaching me in the ways of whitewater.

It's hard to separate the New River of West Virginia from Adventures on the Gorge outfitters and the gracious hospitality of Dave Arnold. An honor to this great river, Jo-Beth Stamm was unconditionally the ultimate guide.

At the Chattooga, I called on two old buddies who had paddled there as stuntmen in a famous film in 1972. Claude Terry was unable to join us, but Doug Woodward, author of *Wherever Waters Flow*, joined us for two days with the company Doug had founded, Southeastern River Expeditions. Defining the word "pro," Geoff Doolittle and Linc Stallings guided us through Sections 3 and 4. In Wisconsin, Denny Caneff arranged for some great river time.

My long-standing pal Bob Banks had joined me for my first megatrip the whole way down the Susquehanna in 1975 and forty years later met up with me to help at the Saint Croix and also at the Yellowstone. For tips there, thanks to the sage expeditioneer and acclaimed author of river-running lore, Al Kesselheim.

At the Arkansas River in Colorado, Bill and Jackie Dvorak of Dvorak Raft, Kayak, and Fishing Expeditions helped us with a week of trips, and Bill, Matt Dvorak, and Matias Flores expertly guided us through the most intense whitewater. Unlike many outfitters who limit their offerings to a single lucrative reach, Bill and Jackie have spent a lifetime hosting people to rivers all across Colorado, including environmental education adventures, and Bill has spent decades in public service leading conservation initiatives and training hundreds of guides and public safety officials in river rescue.

At the Rio Grande, Steve Harris of Far Flung Adventures has been the key outfitter and river steward for two generations. His guides Chris Ledger and Bill Lynch led us through the Middle Box.

For my first run down the Tuolumne, and for invitations so I could row through the Grand Canyon and down the Selway, thanks to the pioneering C-1 paddler and great California conservationist Jerry Meral. Also on the Tuolumne, Bob Ferguson of Zephyr Whitewater Expeditions let me row along with his group led by master guide Noah Triplett. Paul Vanderheiden expertly outfitted my Forks of the Kern trip. Bob Pierce—a beloved elder in Oregon—led the way on my first Rogue and Deschutes trips in 1977, as did Bill Sedivy, former director of Idaho Rivers United, on the Snake River in 2015.

A model of what a river outfitter should be, Zach Collier of Northwest Rafting Company opened his Owyhee journey to me and Ann in our raft. Scott Cushing took a day to lead me down the White Salmon.

Peter Enticknap shared his permit for my second trip down the Tatshenshini. Then my sisterlike cousin Mary Bettencourt and her husband Greg joined Ann and me on the Copper, and our tight little foursome became the most completely simpatico two couples I can imagine. I'll always remember my Sheenjek partners Lou Brown and Jon Miller with exceptional fondness as members of my tribe. Finally, a special callout to veteran river runner Verne Huser, whose guiding and teaching has brought people to rivers across the West for more than half a century.

For reviews of specific river descriptions in this book, thanks to Ken Cline for the rivers of Maine; Bone Bayse of Beaver Brook Outfitters for the Hudson; Carl Paulson of the New Hampshire Rivers Council for the Saco; Julie Bell of the National Park Service for the Delaware; Jerry Walls, Lycoming County Planning Director, for Pine Creek; Steve and Miranda Putt of Country Squirrel Outfitters for the Clarion; Eric Martin of Wilderness Voyagers for the Youghiogheny; Dave Arnold at Adventures on the Gorge for the New and Gauley; Doug Woodward for the Chattooga; Katherine Haney of the Suwannee River Water Management District; guidebook author Don Philpott for the Wekiva; Caven Clark of the National Park Service for the Buffalo; Dena Matheson of the Ozark National Scenic Riverways for the Current;

Randy Ferrin and Steve Johnson of the Saint Croix National Scenic Riverway; Steve Hicks of Fort Niobrara National Wildlife Refuge and Duane Gudgel of the Plains Trading Company for the Niobrara; Sean Reynolds, river ranger on the upper Missouri; Al Kesselheim, wilderness canoeing author, for the Yellowstone; Miles Cottom, former raft guide, for the Arkansas; Dave Cernicek of Bridger-Teton National Forest for the Snake; Bill Sedivy for the rivers of Idaho; Mike Fiebig of American Rivers for the Flathead; Kelly Kager of the National Park Service for the Green, Yampa, and middle Colorado; river runner Darin Martens of the Forest Service for the Green, Yampa, and Grand Canyon; Linda Jalbert, retired from the National Park Service, for the Grand Canyon; Gigi Richard, Mesa University geologist, for the middle Colorado; Steve Harris of Far Flung Adventures for the San Juan and Rio Grande; Jerry Meral for the Tuolumne; Jim Eicher of the BLM for the South Fork American; paddlers Larry Laitner and Karen Salley for the Klamath; Zach Collier of Northwest Rafting Company for the Middle Fork Salmon, Kern, Tuolumne, Owyhee, and White Salmon; Colby Hawkinson, BLM river ranger, for the Rogue; Dean Finnerty, fishing guide and Trout Unlimited staffer at the Umpqua; Travis Williams, guidebook author and director of Willamette Riverkeeper; Jon Benson, BLM river ranger, for the Deschutes; Grant Richie, outfitter on the Grande Ronde; Patrick Kollodge, former John Day river ranger for the BLM; and Karen Jettmar, friend and guidebook author, for Alaska.

Professionals in the care of these rivers are organized as the River Management Society, capably directed by Risa Shimoda. River running in America would be unconscionably diminished in quality without the dedicated service of these resource specialists. Finally, we all owe gratitude and support to a host of river conservation groups that take responsibility for keeping our rivers free-flowing and healthy. For a list of these, contact River Network, American Rivers, and the Waterkeeper Alliance.

TO ANN, AND TO ALL THE RIVERS WE LOVE

First published in the United States of America in 2018 by
Rizzoli International Publications, Inc.
300 Park Avenue South • New York, NY 10010 • www.rizzoliusa.com

Photographs and Text © 2018 Tim Palmer • Foreword © 2018 Richard Bangs

Photographs on pages 4-5, 26-27, 48-49, 162-163, 168-169, 182-183, and 238 (top) were taken by Ann Vileisis.

Associate Publisher: James Muschett • Project Editor: Candice Fehrman • Book Design: Susi Oberhelman

American Rivers protects wild rivers, restores damaged rivers, and conserves clean water for people and nature. Since 1973, American Rivers has protected and restored more than 150,000 miles of rivers through advocacy efforts, on-the-ground projects, and an annual America's Most Endangered Rivers® campaign. To celebrate the fiftieth anniversary of the Wild and Scenic Rivers Act in 2018, American Rivers and its partners have launched 5,000 Miles of Wild—a campaign to protect 5,000 new miles of Wild and Scenic Rivers and one million acres of riverside lands. Headquartered in Washington, DC, American Rivers has offices across the country and more than 275,000 members, supporters, and volunteers. For more information, visit www.AmericanRivers.org.

2018 2019 2020 2021 / 10 9 8 7 6 5 4 3 2 1

Printed in China • ISBN-13: 978-0-8478-6173-6 • Library of Congress Catalog Control Number: 2017954380

CAPTIONS FOR PHOTOS ON THE OPENING PAGES OF THIS BOOK:
PAGE 1: At the Youghiogheny's Cucumber Rapid in Pennsylvania, guide-trainee Marissa Sommers of Wilderness Voyageurs aces the drop with smiles all around. PAGES 2-3: Creating some of the most challenging whitewater in the East, the Chattooga River of Georgia, South Carolina, and North Carolina pounds over sandstone ledges. PAGES 4-5: Enchanting all who paddle on its lucid waters, the Grande Ronde River in Oregon also supports endangered salmon migrating upstream to spawn. PAGES 6-7: The Alsek River pushes with massive volumes of glacial runoff through Alaska's coastal mountain ranges.

Hoh

Skagit

Sauk

WA

White Salmon

Yakima

Snake

Columbia

St. Joe

Clark Fork

Clearwater

N Fk Flathead

Missouri

MT

ND

Willamette

Deschutes

Grande Ronde

Selway

Imnaha

Snake

Salmon

M Fk Salmon

Salmon

Yellowstone

Clarks Fork

Little Missouri

John Day

OR

ID

Owyhee

Snake

Bruneau

Snake

Gros Ventre

Hoback

Bear

WY

SD

White

Missouri

Rogue

Umpqua

Klamath

Smith

Eel

Sacramento

Feather

American

S Fk American

Mokelumne

Tuolumne

Merced

San Joaquin

CA

Kings

N Fk Kern

Humboldt

NV

UT

Green

Colorado

Yampa

White

Colorado

CO

Arkansas

South Platte

Niobrara

Platte

NE

KS

Arkansas

Virgin

San Juan

Colorado

Rio Grande

Cimarron

Malibu Cr

Colorado

Gila

Verde

AZ

Gila

Rio Grande

NM

Rio Grande

Pecos

TX

Brazos

Colville

Noatak

Sheenjek

Porcupine

Koyukuk

Yukon

AK

Yukon

Tanana

Nenana

Kuskokwim

Susitna

Copper

Tatshenshini

Alsek

Chilkat

Brooks

Rio Grande

0   200 Miles